For Stan and
Marilyn Gabor –

with Best
wishes and
in gratitude;

Pieces
of an
Examined
Life

Stephen Vicchio

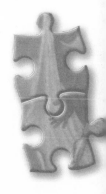

Pieces
of an
Examined
Life

ESSAYS AND STORIES
BY

STEPHEN VICCHIO

WOODHOLME
HOUSE
PUBLISHERS

Baltimore, Maryland

©1999, Stephen Vicchio

First Edition, First Printing

Library of Congress Cataloging-in-Publication Data

Vicchio, Stephen.
Pieces of an examined life : essays and stories / by Stephen Vicchio.
p. cm.
ISBN 1-891521-06-3 (pbk.)
I. Title
AC8.V416   1999
081—dc21   99-13695
                                             CIP

Woodholme House Publishers
131 Village Square I
Village of Cross Keys
Baltimore, Maryland 21210
Orders: 1-800-488-0051
e-mail: gregg@woodholmehouse.com

Book and cover design: Lance Simons
Backcover photograph: Sandra Parsons Vicchio
Cover art: School of Athens, detail of the center showing Plato and Aristotle with students including Michelangelo and Diogenes, 1510-11 (fresco) by Raphael (Raffaello Sanzio of Urbino) (1483-1520)
Vatican Museums and Galleries, Vatican City, Italy/Bridgeman Art Library

For Sandra,
one of God's miracles of beauty

*It is better to be Socrates dissatisfied,
than a pig satisfied.*
John Stuart Mill

CONTENTS

ACKNOWLEDGMENTS

Many of the essays and homilies in this volume had their first appearance elsewhere. I am grateful to the *Baltimore Sun*, *Markings*, *Maryland Magazine*, *Baltimore Magazine*, *The Catholic Review*, *The Baltimore Jewish Times*, and *Style* for their gracious permission to use them here.

Jennifer Shea helped in heroic ways with the preparation of the manuscript. Gregg Wilhelm remains the best editor I could imagine having. Liz and Brian Weese should be applauded here (and other places) for their love of books and their confidence in Baltimore's writers. My colleagues in the philosophy department at the College of Notre Dame continue to find office space and space in their large hearts for me. I am grateful for both.

The past few years have taught me much about how lives can be scattered into pieces, and still more about how they are held together. A number of my friends have helped in countless ways on countless occasions in the latter department, particularly David and Laura Duncan, Jeff and Pat Dayton. It would only be fair to thank them properly here, though I suspect the measure of gratitude I owe them could never be properly repaid. With their gentle friendships I continue to think it all worth writing about.

Goethe in a fine essay on love writes, "We are shaped and fashioned, more than anything else, by what we love." I am blessed to love and be loved by my wife, Sandra, and my son Reed. It is a rare man who is loved as completely as I. My family continues to shape and fashion in large ways, and in subtle ones, what good is to be found in me.

> *The unexamined life is not worth living.*
> Socrates

An Introduction

Pieces of an Examined Life

Methinks I hear him now; his plausive words.
He scatter'd not in ears, but grafted them,
To grow there and to bear.
William Shakespeare
All's Well That Ends Well

Mouths of fire...stream of words...in her ear...
practically in her ear...not catching the half...
not the quarter...
Samuel Beckett
Not I

t is a little known fact among those who do not wield a pen for a living that short occasional essays are called "pieces" in the world of publishing. Rarely will one hear a veteran newspaper person or magazine editor talk about "stories," and still less about "columns." The word is "pieces," and this sense gives the first meaning to the title of this book. Over the past two decades I have written hundreds of pieces for the *Baltimore Sun* and other publications. I have collected many of them in three previous books of essays and short stories.

Since the publication of *The I of the Beholder* in 1995, one could say my life has been in pieces in the sense that Fitzgerald uses the word in *Crack-up*. I have watched as my first marriage ended in divorce. I have watched as my brother became paralyzed in an accident, later to recover his ability to walk. I have watched as my stepson (a term I had never used until this moment) went from being an integral part of my life to someone whom others wished to push to the very edges of it. I have watched as my younger son went from baby to preschooler in a magical transformation worthy of Ovid's *Metamorphosis*. And I have watched love bloom within me again, thanks to an extraordinary woman.

Along the way, my professional life has become increasingly more complicated, even fragmented. I seem to do more things, in less time than I ever have—a malady, I suspect, of nearly all in this country who live and work at the end of the millennium. I struggle to keep the edges of the puzzle in place, while, in the interior, the pieces often seem to have minds of their own.

More than anything, this book acts as a kind of record of what I have been thinking and feeling over the past few years. It is a catalogue of my likes and dislikes, some might say prejudices, both for and against. About half these pieces come in the form of the personal essay, some are written as homilies, and about twenty pieces are short fiction.

No matter what the form, most of these pieces come from somewhere pretty close to the bone. I have written here of days on the beach with my young son; the stillness of October afternoons; the difficulties of being evicted from step-parenting; and the reactions of a strong family when tragedy strikes. In other pieces I try to get to the heart of hypocrisy, suffering, and forgiveness. I explore the nature of my faith, and the beliefs and religious struggles of those with whom I share much of my life. I posit a few notions about men losing their hair, the nature of time, and the secrets of college.

The short stories in this volume have not been published elsewhere. Several of these fictional pieces grew out of encounters with the works of Soren Kierkegaard, Leo Tolstoy, Franz Kafka, Anton Chekhov, and a number of the Chinese Classics. They are best understood, I think, as parables, not all that different from the gospel variety.

George Santayana in one of his letters points out that to do philosophy well, you must spend a life time, thinking it, teaching it, and when the spirit moves you, writing it, whether it shows up in academic journals, in novels and short stories, or where it simply provides amusement for family and friends. For better or worse, I have devoted my adult life to the teaching and writing of philosophy. I think of this book as an extension of that writing and teaching, and learning as well. In one of his finest dialogues, Plato has his mentor Socrates tell us that "the unexamined life is not worth living." But in the same dialogue, Socrates wryly informs us that "the wise man is the man who knows he knows nothing." I have spent my adult life examining my life, and those of others, looking for this elusive wisdom.

SJV
Christmas, 1998
Baltimore

In order to improve the mind, we ought
Less to learn, than to contemplate.
Rene Descartes
Meditations

Chapter 1

Less to Learn,
Than to Contemplate

Taking Note of Time

*In theory one is aware that the earth
revolves but in practice one does not
perceive it. The ground on which one
treads seems not to move, and one can
live undisturbed. So it is with Time
in one's life.*

Marcel Proust
Remembrance of Things Past

We take no note of time, but from its loss.

Owen Young
Letters

We have spun back to this spot. We have hurtled headlong through space, until we are back where we began. It is the end of the year. If Medieval monks had been a bit more adept, a tad more accurate at marking the birth of Christ, it might also have been the end of the millennium, and the beginning.

A confused housefly hurls itself repeatedly against the window panes of my study. After too many attempts at escape, it falls exhausted and faintly buzzes among the EXs of my open *Oxford English Dictionary*. It lies on its back, doing strange clockwise circles on the page. The buzzing continues more faintly until the fly dies in the margin, just a few body lengths from "exit" and "expire," on the same page as "expendable."

The fly has managed a bit of poetry, what some might call performance art, in the end of its life, but it is unconscious poetry, the curious happenstance of the right space and running out of time. My dear mother warned us as children about such happenstance. That is why she thought it so important, at all times, to wear clean underwear. She had a finely tuned sense of the tragic possibilities of life, and she wanted us to be dressed for the occasion.

The eighteenth century letters of Owen Young have me thinking this morning that it is only at the ends of things that time becomes visible. Space is always in sight, even in one's dreams, but time is usually invisible, silent, unless it is accompanied by weeping. Space forces the eye to follow it, while time's movement is secretly gauged by the heart, or in the pocketbook.

It is a curious and little observed fact that the human mind does not measure time the way the calendar does. The police might ask a suspect, "Where were you on the evening of March 21, 1993?" But the mind thinks of it as the night that Michael Jordan scored sixty points, or a friend had a memorable birthday party. The human mind seems to need hooks on which to hang time. Without those hooks, the numbers mean little.

In early Roman times, before they had their own names for the gods, Chronos was portrayed as having two separate pairs of wings. One set was outstretched as if about to take flight, while the other pair, paradoxically, was lowered for landing. It is only at year's end, or life's end, or the end of anything that is good, that these images can be understood together—time is both the cradle of hope and the grave of ambition. Perhaps this is why we schedule our mid-life crises two-thirds of the way along our allotted time. We cannot bear to think about the end until it is time. If time is a "maniac scattering dust," it is only when his bag is empty that we pay him any notice. Apparently, we are content to give the maniac a few more years of sprinkling before we declare the millennium has come.

When the bag is nearly empty, time becomes clear. It is then we try to put knots in the rope of time, but they are more like the magician's knots that mysteriously disappear in our hands. They fall through our fingers. They end up in that place where there is no time.

At year's end we try vainly to drive a nail through time, to fix it in place the way we might mistakenly attempt to keep a spinning gyroscope in one spot. But the gyroscope and the earth do their spinning, and the millennium approaches, or, it is about to pass.

Only time can turn a dictionary into a graveyard. Only we notice it.

On Walking

Early this morning the longing for a walk has stirred my winter-buried life. It takes a few minutes to find the proper shoes in the back of my newly cluttered closet, and then I am gone.

I did not walk in my former neighborhood. There were no side-walks there, and motorists on their way to the strip mall might not have paid enough attention to a peripatetic philosopher to make it safe for a stroll, so I confined myself to walking on my suburban property. These, of course, were not walks at all. They fulfilled one of the requirements of a proper walk (that one explore the self), but not the other (finding out about the neighborhood). Moving back to the city a few months ago, I have recovered the real elements of a walking life.

Sometime over the past six years of life in the suburbs I had lost my will to walk. I was no special case. At the close of the millennium, we in this country generally are unwilling walkers. We are not the innocent, simple-hearted souls our grandparents were. They walked everywhere—and when they were not walking with a purpose, they walked simply for the joy of walking. We who live at the end of their century have fallen from our grandparents' state of grace, and one of the principal signs of our lapsed natures is our incapacity to enjoy a good walk.

My generation seems also to be going somewhere in a car. Along the way we have lost the pleasures of walking. One of these is surely a renewed interest in the particularity of things. But through the windshield of an automobile we lose the singular nature of life: one daffodil among many; a single drifting cloud; or a solitary wind-aided ripple moving across a tiny man-made pond in the neighborhood.

In traffic we function as disconnected atoms, all parts of an unwitting but growing chaos. Our lives are made empty by their continued fullness. Always on the move, our lives are reduced to monotony by the sheer variety of places we might drive. We differ from our grandparents not only in our responses but also in our lack of time to respond. Our field of vision has been partly defined by what we are made blind to. What has died in us, or what is dying in us, sheds an eerie light—like the high beams of head lights in a fog—on that which remains only partially alive in us. And so, in this tardy spring I have had to relearn how to walk, and to see. I had forgotten, for example, that one must be prepared on a walk to lose one's way, or to have no way at all. Walks are not the same as trips.

Before my first few walks I did not remember the smells on an unhurried stroll, how they rush upon us and then dissipate like a breaking wave. I did not recall that when taking a walk one should not be accompanied by small children, for they see too much. I had forgotten the value of walking at night. When one is anxious or worried about the world, or simply one's small place in it, a salve sometimes can be found in the night air. I did not remember how therapeutic it can be when one is lonely or fearful to scowl at the darkness.

More than anything else, in my new-found walking I have come to two important understandings. First, that every walk is a journey. No traveler remains untouched, even when the journey is a short one. And finally, there is a great value in meandering. All those who wander are not lost.

October Afternoon

The summer fades and passes, and
October comes. We'll smell smoke
then, and feel an unsuspected sharpness,
a thrill of nervousness, swift elation,
a sense of sadness and departure.
Thomas Wolfe
You Can't Go Home Again

We fall to rise, are baffled to fight better. Sleep to wake.
Robert Browning
Asalando

Summer light fades in an October afternoon the way love is often lost. It disappears over a hillside that, only moments before, seemed green and verdant, but now is dark and sear. Trees drop their leaves, like something whispered just out of the range of hearing. The leaves release their grasp on mother trees. They lose their strength in ones and twos. In their brief afterlife, they might swirl together and chase a transit bus, or lie alone on the damp and fading grass.

Among the ancient Chinese the leaf was a symbol of happiness. Leaves clustered together stood for a human community: distinct individuals but joined in a complex system of connection and nourishment. Only the Chinese could invent such a metaphor. It was a way of dispelling autumnal loneliness.

We have entered the season of forgetting and remembering. The sun pauses briefly in its decay. In the hollow of the early autumn, late afternoon, young mothers congregate around the tiny ponds near my

1

home. They speak of stretch marks and tuition. With one eye on the conversation, they set their children free to find handfuls of unripe acorns and chestnuts.

A surprisingly stiff wind picks up across the ponds, and the ducks resettle their feathers. In a few weeks they will be gone. The mothers turn up the collars of their jackets and crowd together like thistles, but the children do not notice the turning of the wind.

Such a fall afternoon at dusk can make things so clear. Low clouds move shadows across the ponds. Something is pushing us all toward winter. The earth changes and it does not pause for our permission. It makes us all live surrounded by the air of baffled existence. It is only the winter that will decide if it may ignore our need for warmth.

Walking from the park, my eye meets those of one of the mothers. My memory quickly unlooses a gallery of faces, but the woman's is not among them. Her eyes just as quickly consult memory, I pause, but she does not return my greeting. In the air there is the pungent smell of leaves on fire.

On the edge of the park, I stop to look back at the ponds, and the branch of a small birch brushes against my face, losing some of its yellow leaves. I remember Orlando's line in *As You Like It*:

Under the shade of melancholy boughs,
Lose and neglect the creeping hours of time.

In a late October afternoon, on the path leading back to my home, I remember an old Chinese proverb: time is the echo of leaves falling.

VAGARIES

*What mockeries are our firm resolves—to will is ours,
but not to execute. We map our futures like some
unknown coast, and say here is a harbor, there is a
rock; the one we will attain, the other shun, and we
do neither; some chance gale springs up, and bears us
o'er some unfathomable sea.*

L.E. Landon

Essays

*Chance is always powerful—
Let your hook be cast;
In the pool where you least expect it,
there will be a fish.*

Ovid

Metamorphosis

A s a child on my way to Catholic grade school, I passed every day
a cardboard sign held together by two-by-fours and a smaller
piece of wood that was placed diagonally on the back of the sign.
The sign was sunk into the ground at the corner of the church property. It swayed perceptibly in a stiff wind. Across the street was a
cemetery.

On the front of the sign in tall black letters it read: "Bingo
Thursday." By the time I was a third grader, already I had passed the
sign some twelve hundred times, but it only occurred to me by the
end of that year that the sign did not say "Bingo Thursday, if things
work out," nor even "Bingo, God willing." No, the sign proudly proclaimed, with what struck me at the time as enormous hubris, that

9

two things were inevitable. First, that there would be a Thursday. And second, that bingo would be played that day. The makers of the sign seemed to make these assertions with the same kind of surety that God employed in knowing next year's winner of the Irish Sweepstakes. But even at the age of seven, I did not share their confidence.

I remember walking home from school, my blue duffel bag dragging behind me, wondering how the makers of the sign could be so sure about Thursday bingo, or anything else for that matter. Hadn't the nuns said the world would one day come to an end? Wasn't it the case that we were taught to wear clean underwear, precisely so we would be prepared for just such emergencies?

It is helpful to remember the context in which my seven-year-old mind turned to the vagaries of life. These third grade experiences occurred within the larger backdrop of the 1950s, a time when there were enough nuclear arms aimed our way that it was certainly possible that in a moment's notice Thursday could be canceled. The 1950s were a time when my parents' friends hid Christmas presents in their bomb shelters.

These days any musings about the transitory nature of life has little to do with geopolitics or nuclear physics. By the time one has reached middle-age, the entire sweep of history is no longer one's purview. The vagaries of one's own life are usually more than enough to keep one busy.

By going some place a few moments earlier or later, by stopping to tie one's shoe strings, by turning down this street rather than the proper one, or failing to knock loud enough for someone to hear, these all irrevocably may change the course of our lives. And yet, we are so often oblivious to the shape and the texture of these alternative courses.

Perhaps more than any other day, for Christians Christmas is a time when we attempt to ward off chance, to assert that there is some sort of deep, divine sense to the way things work. Whether it is the childhood belief that good people get presents and bad people do not, or it is the adult assertion that God sent a son to die for our sins, there is in the season, always just below the surface, the enormous human will to make things make sense.

Amongst the gift-giving, the holiday parties, and the frenzied rush to find the one present that will convince the other of our faithfulness, there is the understanding, at least for believers, that in this season we begin to draw a wide circle, the circumference of which is completed on Easter Sunday. Along the way, we will be treated to the vagaries of life, but in the making of the circle we are asserting that life takes us somewhere—that life is not a careless arrow shot into the darkness. In this season of chance we dare to claim that the meaning of things starts with the birth a of tiny child in a manger full of soiled straw, and that God has not forgotten human need.

THE NIGHT WATCHERS

I am become a borrower of the night.
For a dark hour or twain.
William Shakespeare
Macbeth

If I must die
I will encounter the darkness as a bride,
and hug it in mine arms.
William Shakespeare
Measure for Measure

I am a man who usually finds shadows far more interesting than the objects that cast them. Perhaps this is why I always have loved the night. The blacker the better. T.S. Eliot tells us that "midnight shakes the memory." In the dead of night, the slats of the mind move closer together, little falls between the cracks. The night pushes thought inward; it moves the soul to envelope back upon itself.

There is a grandeur and tranquility in the darkest of nights. It becomes a time devoted to mental arithmetic, some adding, but mostly subtracting. It is a time for listening to sand frantically running through an invisible hourglass. The city heaves and sighs. It rolls over on its other ear a few times and falls soundly to sleep. The world is left to be knitted together by those of us who remain its thinking reeds. In the darkest of nights solitude need not be sought. It is as close as nakedness. When night closes the eyes of the city, it opens as many within its night watchers.

This evening I am left alone to think about hope. In these dark moments it finally becomes clear to me that hope is nothing more than falling in love with a life one does not have. If hope is a thing with feathers, its wings are black, its twin is fear.

But sometimes even twins go their separate ways. This evening, sleep has been turned cold by recurrent dreams. I am awake now, and I am hoping about the dead. A small, tight circle of light is cast over me and my writing desk. Beyond that is only darkness.

I am thinking about a Rilke poem that insists that the living are but trees who bear the sweet fruit of death. We are simply husk and leaf, part of the mud and the motion of a tiny, and perhaps forgotten, planet.

Edward Gibbon when asked shortly before his death whether he considered it desirable to think of death as a long sleep, answered rather emphatically, "Yes, provided one could be sure of the dreams."

This evening, in the dead of night, I am trying to be sure about the dreams. I am hoping that somewhere the dead hold hands in a communion of saints. This evening, in the dark, I have risen from bed to be taken hold of by a hope that life is larger than the vessel in which it is kept.

In the morning, the natural light with strengthen, and the remainder of the room again will take shape. A moment or two later the stark yellow light will bathe the foreheads of the houses across the way, and thoughts of the dead will dissipate in the morning mist that rises from autumn lawns.

But tonight I write—just in case we are only vegetable mold. I write in the middle of the night, and I hope for something that lasts—what Keats once bent to learn, painted forever on a certain urn.

THE HEART OF THE UNIVERSE

*Cease not to think of the universe as one
living Being, possessed of a single substance
and a single mind and heart.*

Marcus Aurelius
Meditations

*The whole universe together participates
in the divine goodness more perfectly and
represents it better than any single creature
whatever.*

Thomas Aquinas
Summa Theologica

M y physicist friends tell me that one version of the Big Bang theory suggests that the universe exploded out of a tiny compressed
dot of immensely heavy matter and will forever expand—a kind
of relentless, cosmic one-shot deal—an open-ended game of chance
where Providence always has time for one more roll of the dice.

A rival theory has it that the universe does indeed expand, but
then, after eons of spreading itself slowly over nothingness, it col-
lapses again into the dense chaos from which the Big Bang came.
There are few metaphors to be employed in explaining the former
theory, but in this latter view of things all that there is undergoes a
never-ending cycle of expansion and contraction, like the opening
and closing of a human hand, or the constricting and relaxing of the
human heart.

I must admit to my preference for this second theory. We humans
seem forever to be attempting to make the entire universe into a

macrocosm of our most fervent wants and desires of the heart. This is why we read tea leaves and build cyclotrons. It would be of some great solace to believe, particularly on the feast of Saint Valentine, that the universe wishes to return the favor by making each of us a microcosm of itself.

The seventeenth century philosopher and telescope lens grinder Baruch Spinoza must have searched for the same kind of spiritual and emotional reassurance. This is why he describes the entire universe as the beating heart of God, and each of our individual hearts as possessing a unitary desire to be at one with God's great heart. Albert Einstein spoke of the real purpose of science as an attempt at hearing the heartbeat of God. Meister Eckhardt, the fourteenth century Dominican church builder and mystic, had the same vision. He wrote that our hearts are all connected, like the single-mindedness of migratory birds, in a desire to be connected to the heart of the universe itself. He was branded a heretic long after he died. Now it is my turn.

In our small corner of the universe where love so often seems absent, and having lived a life, now deep into middle age, with too much love lost and not nearly enough saved, it would be of great comfort to know that the entire universe is nothing more than a big heart beating deep in the chest of a mysterious and loving Void.

We all at times have lived with hearts as dry as the desert, never thinking to ask where the next watering hole might be. We all have waited impatiently for the hearts of stones to awaken. Most of us have lived among hearts frozen thick, like lake ice in a Minnesota February. Many of us too unwisely have worn naked hopes before these immobile hearts, freeze-dried by anger and disappointment. At times, we all have ceased to believe in the existence of spring.

And so, on Saint Valentine's Day let us remember this curious saint whose heart seems to have been warmed by virtue of a secret and mysterious fire, a heart as loving as it is mysterious—a heart perhaps as large as the universe itself. And on this feast of Saint Valentine's Day let us root for a theory of the universe that might help us to think of our frozen winter as a temporary state, one perhaps only overcome by the warmest of hearts.

Man is the merriest species;
all above or below are serious.
Joseph Addison
Essays

Chapter 2

The Merriest Species

THE PARTY IN MY BEDROOM CLOSET

*It was then that I first learned to know
the influence that can emanate directly
from beyond the door of an open clothes closet.*
Rainer Maria Rilke
The Notebooks of Malte Laurids Brigge

I suspect that odd things are going on in my bedroom closet when I am not around. The psychology of closets is very different than other rooms in the house. They make us uneasy. They reach into some limbic part of us, primitive, dark, and inexplicable. That's why we hide things there. That is why gay people think it is a good idea to come out of the closet. That's why we shut our closet doors at night.

My bedroom closet is an unbridled place. It has not been subdued like the rest of my house. Indeed, when I venture into my bedroom closet, I feel as though whatever has been going on a moment ago has just stopped dead. It's like one of those old Larson cartoons, where cows are standing on their hind legs hoisting Martini glasses to each other in one frame, followed by a second panel in which one of the cows is shouting "Car!" whereupon all the cows move to all fours, only to resume their partying in the final frame after the uninvited guest has driven by. This is why my closet makes me nervous. I know something subversive is going on in there.

I have long suspected that my bedroom closet really doesn't belong to me. It may well belong to the rest of the bedroom. We can enter a closet but we do not live or belong there for any length of time. I know all this sounds like the ravings of a madman, or perhaps someone who has read Rilke's *Notebooks* a few too many times, but the point may become clear by offering an experiment.

Go into your bedroom closet and close the door behind you. Notice how the clothes press against you. They are unwilling to give up their space to an intruder. They may have been intimate with you in the past, but now they ignore you. The snub is embarrassing. They much prefer to be among their own kind. The clothes go there to get away from you. It is the retreat they find when they no longer wish to smell like you. And when you surprise them and enter the closet unannounced they are never happy to see you. In fact, the silence that inevitably accompanies your unexpected intrusion is eerily similar to the embarrassed silence of friends who you know just moments before have been talking unkindly about you.

The other clear reason for arguing that you really don't own your closet is the unassailable proposition that you have no idea what is actually in there. Think about the last time you moved. Do you remember all the surprising things you found in the back of your bedroom closet? Do you remember wondering how much of it got there? It is because some of that stuff has been invited over by your shoes. I know they seem to sit there all paired off behaving themselves, but I have detected the faintest twitch of a shoe lace upon yanking open the closet door.

The closet, of course, may be the real location of Freud's unconscious. Perhaps for married folks it is a collective unconscious. Repression is just another name for putting ugly things away that nice people ought not to get a good look at. In this sense, the closet does belong to you, but you wish that much of the stuff stashed there didn't. Perhaps we have stumbled on to something here. Wouldn't it be wonderful if God has provided some kind of Cosmic Good Will or a Psychological Salvation Army where we could take those contents of our unconscious that we no longer thought of as useful to us. Various second-hand feelings of inferiority might be just what the doctor ordered for some person with an inflated ego browsing for a good buy.

THE ROUNDNESS OF THE EARTH

What better way, then, to judge the sanity of
a man than to measure his pronouncements
about the world against how well they correspond
to the way the world is.
Sigmund Freud
Letters

I believe that there are certain doors which only
illness can open. There is a certain state of health
that does not allow us to understand everything;
and perhaps illness shuts us off from certain truths;
but health shuts us off just as effectively from others,
or turns us away from them so that they are no longer
of our concern.
Andre Gide
The Journals

When Michael leapt from the third floor hospital window, he felt for the first time what it meant to be absolutely free. As he jumped his knees bent, and he flapped his arms furiously the way a baby bird might in a first attempt at flight. His landing was not nearly as soft as he mentally had rehearsed it. While in his short flight, a fall really, he had imagined himself a great bird, perhaps a noble eagle or a giant white dove. Just as he leapt he made a little sound, "Caw....caw..." But he landed with a thud, more like a two-hundred pound, forty-five-year-old mental patient, desperate to escape, than the bald symbol of a great nation or a sleek, white-feathered embodiment of the Holy Spirit.

At first, he kept to the woods that lined the hospital road. He moved deliberately, stopping behind large naked trees when he saw head lights approaching the buildings on the far side of the hospital property. By the time he came to the edge of the hospital grounds, he moved swiftly, purposefully, from tree to tree. When he arrived at the large iron gate, he hoisted himself over it, the back of his brown corduroy coat momentarily getting stuck on one of the sharp spear-like protrusions at the top of the gate.

For a moment, he hung there, arms akimbo, looking a little like Jesus on the cross, or perhaps a marionette hanging lifelessly from the side of a magic box. Then he braced the heels of his brown Oxfords against the iron gate and with a mighty grunt Michael tore himself free from his confinement. As he did, he sang the words of a Negro spiritual, "Free at last...free at last. Thank God almighty...I'm free at last."

On the other side of the gate, he remembered Arnold's advice, which he had received in exchange for two cigarettes in the most important aside of an otherwise boring group-therapy session last Tuesday. Arnold had escaped many times and knew as much about the logic of life lived in town as anybody in the hospital—doctor or patient. Arnold had told him about the loose bars in the window of the third floor men's room on B2. He had accepted the smokes from Michael, knowing the younger man had little chance of making it. "Still, a deal is a deal," Arnold thought, "even among crazy people."

While Frank, a small man with red hair and a bi-polar disorder, was talking about how his sister had fastened a garden hose to the tail pipe of her Volvo and ran it to the front window so that she might quietly and bloodlessly kill herself, Arnold nudged Michael, the way one might communicate in church or at a funeral home. "When you come to town," Arnold whispered, "before you do anything, you need to convince them of your sanity. You should talk only about things that you are absolutely certain. If you have any doubts, keep the comment to yourself, otherwise, this will be a very short trip. You'll give yourself away, and those sonofabitches in the white coats will drag you back here in a New York minute."

As he walked along in the dark following the lights toward town, Michael thought about Arnold's advice, and about how much better the air smelled on the outside. He stopped for a moment and inhaled as deeply as he could, a broad smile forming on his thick lips.

At the far edge of the woods, he found a small rubber ball lying in the snow. It was the kind of ball usually connected by an elastic string to a wooden paddle, but neither the paddle nor the tether were to be found. Michael placed the rubber ball in his coat pocket. With every step he took the ball gently struck him in the left leg, and he said aloud, as if rehearsing for something, "Bang, the earth is round. Bang, the earth is round."

When Michael arrived at the Double-B Diner a mile or so from the iron hospital gate, it was empty, except for Miss Hare, the counter waitress, and Louis Flag, a United States Postal worker, a man with whom Michael had shared the mysteries of quadratic equations thirty years earlier with Father Cahill, a Jesuit priest, the owner of a deep, tubercular cough and tobacco stained fingers on his consecration hand. The two younger men had been classmates at Mount St. Mary's High School, a second-tier boy's Catholic high school farther in town.

Michael joined Louis Flag at the red swivel stools. He wanted to say something that was absolutely certain, so he ordered a cup of coffee, black, from Miss Hare, and, while she turned her attention to the percolator, Michael looked Louis Flag square in the eye, felt for the rubber ball in his left hip pocket, and then said in as convincing a tone as possible, "You know Louis, the earth is round."

A moment later, Michael took one of the long straws from the silver-top glass container on the counter. He bent the straw into the form of an isosceles triangle, folding the tips of it into either end.

"You know," Michael said with all the strained casualness of a first date, "perhaps you will remember that the interior angles of a triangle are equal to one hundred and eighty degrees."

For his part, Louis Flag did not know quite what to do. He had not liked Michael when he was sane. In high school Louis had reached his life's peak. He had been an athlete and a respectably good student. He had understood most of his adult life as a fall from grace, as being kicked out of the paradisal life of high school. Michael had been a jerk-off in high school. The crazy Michael, at least in the considered opinion of Louis Flagg, was no great improvement over the quirky, unpredictable, and sometimes troubled and violent adolescent Michael had once been. Nevertheless, while his eyes told Miss Hare to use the pay phone around the corner by the ladies' room to call the authorities, Louis kept his former classmate occupied. But almost immediately Michael sensed things were not going well, the way a man at a Rotary meeting knows he will not be re-elected to the office of recording secretary.

Michael looked intently at Louis Flag, while the postman lighted a cigarette. The blue smoke swirled for a moment, giving the postman a new, almost mysterious look. "The surgeon general has determined that cigarette smoking is hazardous to your health," Michael exclaimed in as cheery a voice as possible. Louis Flag abruptly exhaled and then bent the cigarette in the glass ashtray as he watched Miss Hare complete her call.

Michael sensed that the pressure was on, so again he looked Louis square in the eye. "The Green Bay Packers were the winners of the first Super Bowl; one begins tuning a mandolin with an A; normally the adult human being has thirty-two teeth; Thorozine remains an effective treatment for certain forms of schizophrenia; and...one more thing...the integer, seven?...The only whole number between six and eight." He winked at Louis Flag.

When the orderlies came through the diner's front door, they were accompanied by two hospital security guards and a uniformed Baltimore County police officer. The two orderlies had been interrupted while they were on break, so neither was very happy about making the run. They were gruff with Michael, particularly Clarence, a large black man with the Greek letter 'Epsilon' burned into the bicep of his right arm. Clarence was in the habit of reading his horoscope while on his mid-evening break. Patients and orderlies alike knew not to bother him on his break. Clarence frequently bummed cigarettes from Michael. Clarence had been arrested on three different occasions for beating up his wife. Clarence had been through the anger management seminar two times. Michael made a mental note that he had supplied Clarence with smokes for the last time.

The ride back to the hospital was a bumpy and difficult one for Michael. The orderlies had come for him in what looked like a police paddy wagon, with the exception of the word "hospital" written on the side of the truck. It was the same truck they used when patients died. They used it to transport the bodies to the Jenkins Funeral Home, just a few blocks up the same road the hospital is on.

Clarence and the other orderly, Milton, a shorter black man with a gold tooth, had forced Michael to sit in the locked part of the wagon. They had joked with the police officer about how many of the escaped mental patients make their way to the Double-B Diner. Considering the food, they said, escape to the diner was reason enough to take them back to the nut house. Just before they left, Clarence bummed a cigarette from the cop, a round man on whose face gravity and tragedy had conspired to make him old before his time. By the time he had been returned to the ward, Michael already had begun to plot his next great escape.

Later in the evening, when he found Arnold in the television room, the older man was watching "The Wheel of Fortune." Arnold did not particularly like the show, but lately Vanna had played a significant role in his nocturnal fantasy life. Michael told Arnold how ineffective his advice had been. They argued for a few moments until Arnold returned the two smokes he earlier had made in the deal. Later that night, while trying to fall asleep, Michael was tortured by a new conundrum. On his next escape to town, what method would he employ to establish his sanity? What would he say to prove he was firmly in touch with reality? Surely, he would not be expected to say that the world is flat.

That would be crazy indeed.

The Gods' Laughter

Every man is important if he loses his life; and every man is funny if he loses his hat and has to run after it.
G.K. Chesterton
The Everlasting Man

The difference between heaven and hell might well be a matter of perspective.
Jean-Paul Sartre
Letters

I t was a bit like something you might find in the New Age section of the bookstore—the nook inhabited by people who have been touched by angels, and other folks regularly embraced by the light. It was an Elisabeth Kubler-Ross kind of moment, if you know what I mean. A genuine Shirley MacLain kind of thing, with all the spiritual bells and paranormal whistles.

Actually, it was more like something in the supermarket tabloids, perhaps right next to "Nanny Fran leaves Hubby Twelve Years After Rape," "Woman Gives Birth to 200 Pound Son," or "Vanna Still Tortured About Dad's Death."

It would be in thirty-point type and appear in a box above the fold: "I DIED, see p. 6."

When the car hit the bridge, George apparently had not applied the brakes. Later the police—members of the accident reconstruction unit—while munching on their white powder jelly donuts, would wonder why there were no skid marks left on the roadway, nor on the bridge. When they leaned out over the bridge, working out in their minds what had happened, they dropped white powder sugar into the water below. They all agreed, It was not your usual one car fatality.

At first all George saw was a strange green light that turned red, then bible black. The car flipped over like a stiff version of a one and a half gainer, without the pike position. For a moment there was nothing, then he saw his body, as if from a distance, from a vantage point slightly above and to the left of the driver's side, which was now more than half submerged in the dark water and blue moon light.

In another instant, George found himself back in his body, then there was a sound like the crashing of cymbals, followed by what seemed like the whir of an electric drill, and again he felt himself leaving, the way a silk handkerchief might be pulled from the corner of a trouser pocket. Next he felt himself sucked down a long tunnel, like one might imagine a hapless ground crew member accidentally being pulled along with his little orange-cone flashlights into the rotors of a jet engine.

The tunnel ended in a great yellow light, which pulsed, growing greater and smaller like a throbbing headache. He was forced through the light, the way a small plane breaks the thick cloud cover, or a baby is forced through the birth canal into the glare of the delivery room. There was a great clanging noise, like giant steel doors being opened and slammed shut, and then finally what sounded like papers shuffling.

The first to greet George was Mercury, followed by Pan and then Dionysius who was smeared with blood, or perhaps grape jelly. A short distance away thousands of other gods sat in assembly, in what looked like the ruins of an ancient amphitheater, or possibly the fifth century Athenians' Olympic stadium, fallen in disrepair. The gods all were there, as if they had been waiting patiently for George's arrival. Expectations swirled through the celestial crowd like a sacred mist.

"Now that you have arrived in this place," Mercury announced, electrical current coursing between his bushy eyebrows, "it is customary that by special grace you be granted the privilege of making one wish."

"Wilt thou," the god said gravely, "like Tithonus or dear Helen, have eternal youth or beauty, or the most engaging wit? Would you care to have, as Apollo did, the most beautiful woman, or, like Socrates, Plato, or Aristotle the greatest of wisdom among your kind?

Or do you desire any of the other glories the gods keep in this special box?"

He moved to open an ornate chest, what might at one time have been a companion piece to Pandora's box. As he opened the box slowly, Mercury looked back expectantly at George.

"You must choose one, but only one thing," the god intoned, adding a curious emphasis when he repeated the word "one."

George thought for a moment. As he fingered the gash above his right eyebrow, George reflected on the life that had led to this place, to this time beyond time. He thought about how he had endured for so long as the object of others' amusements. He thought back to the countless times he had been the brunt of others' jokes, first in his lonely and neurotic childhood, in his luckless college years, and then later in his hapless marriage. He thought about the scores he had always wanted to settle, the derision that had become a natural part of his sorry existence back on earth, the bullying he had so often endured from so many quarters, and then, slowly, he gathered himself to his full height, took a deep cosmic breath and filled his lungs with what seemed like new courage. Then George addressed the assembled gods.

"Illustrious ladies and gentlemen, eternal members of the celestial abodes, my dear esteemed immortals—I choose for myself this one thing—that for all eternity I always will have others laugh with me and not at me. I wish from you my new and perpetual compatriots to have forever the laugh on my side."

For an instant, not one of the gods made a move, nor did they utter a sound. Instead, they stared blankly at each other and then back at the man. For the longest moment, no one in heaven blinked. All the clocks in heaven stopped their gentle ticking. The light ethereal breeze that usually cooled the heavens had stopped dead in its celestial tracks.

Finally, Apollo began to chuckle. It started as a small rumble, really, what might have been minor stomach trouble if he were mortal. Then he burst out laughing, a piece of holy spittle flying from his cosmic mouth. It landed on his dazzling toga, immediately evaporating. A moment later Athena and Thor were doubled over in laughter.

In an instant they were joined by Uranus, Aphrodite, and then Ahura Mazda, who could not control himself. Then it struck Vishnu as hilarious, as it did the Great Baal, Zeus, and the sons of Gaea, who all had tears of joy in their many eyes. The mirth spread rapidly to Osiris and to the Bodhisattvas who had stopped by for the show.

Before long, the entire place was roiling with laughter, even those in the cheapest seats, the unbaptized babies and their companions, the patient and noble savages. Gods, angels, and immortal souls alike, all were laughing, some slapping each other on their backs, some wiping the tears from their immortal eyes, and some holding their eternal breaths to rid themselves of the hiccups brought on by the laughter. It was as if a decree silently had been passed that all who had died, and all who could not die, must laugh forever.

For the briefest of moments—a moment that might seem like an eternity if the gods were mortal—George, furrowing his wounded brow, wondered if he were in heaven or in hell. Just then his wound began to bleed a bit. He nervously touched the side of his forehead. But then a moment later he concluded that his wish indeed had been granted, and he began to chuckle as well.

Indeed, he assumed that the gods had only the finest senses of humor, and thus it would hardly have been suitable for them to have announced gravely, "Thy wish is granted." If the laugh was always to be on his side, what better way for the gods to show it? For the first time in his existence, George thought of himself as being on the inside of great understanding, as having an appreciation of great irony, something that always had escaped him in the past.

But the laughter continued throughout the day. The man continued to laugh robustly, and so did the gods. Forever.

Hair Today

Hair today, gone tomorrow, you say, and
give a solitary little smile. Yet you know it
is the joke and not the hair that is on you.
Steady. You will look on the bright side.
Good riddance, you say. Think of Absalom
hanging by his hair from a tree. No such
infringement for you. And what of Samson?
Oh God, Samson you say weakly, and read
in the pattern of those hairs in the sink, the
clarion message of power failure.
Richard Selzer
"Bald!" in *Mortal Lessons*

There is something oddly optimistic about referring to Americans in their mid-forties to late fifties as "middle aged." Nowhere else in the world is such a term used consistently for people who already have spent two-thirds of their allotted upright time on the planet. I realize that math scores are plummeting in this country, but aren't our projected life-spans a matter of simple arithmetic?

It comes as no surprise, then, that it is usually at the onset of "middle-age" that people in this country begin to color their hair, and sometimes, in the case of men, to grow the hair they do have as long on one side as necessary so they can effect a flip, usually going east and west, but sometimes coming up from the south, all in the service of covering the obvious.

I should confess that I have a full head of hair well on its way to going completely gray. I have no intention to do anything with my hair, or the rest of me for that matter, other than letting nature take its course, and perhaps clipping a few recalcitrant ear and nose hairs every now and then—what the woman who cuts my hair calls "Middle-Age Man's Maintenance."

If I were going bald, however, I doubt that I would have the good sense, nor the courage, to avoid the flip. What I do know is that I would pick flipping over plugs any day. They look so painful. And don't they know that the rest of us know? Perhaps if you were really tall, and never sat down, you could get away with it. Otherwise, why bother? The use of drugs to re-stimulate hair growth would seem to make more sense, but it is difficult to believe it works as well as those bushy-haired "before and after" guys on cable television would have us think. Mr. Ray notwithstanding, the hair-weave approach would seem to require too much maintenance. And who wants to live his life in constant fear that an unforeseen stiff wind might blow one's cover?

Perhaps the most interesting question about Rogaine, toupees, plugs, hair weaves, and flipping is why so many American men do it. The answer to this question most likely comes in the plural. It has to do with long-standing cultural expectations, with individual and collective desires, both conscious and unconscious.

Homo sapiens of both genders have been beguiled by and have worried about the gain and loss, the comings and tragic goings of hair, throughout recorded history. Samson's strength resided in his hair; Frankish kings and Aztecs priests were forbidden to cut their hair because it was a symbol of their power and holiness; and wigs were used by ancient Sumerian holy men to ward off evil and treacherous spirits.

In Africa the shorn head was associated with slavery, as it was in China, Burma, in nineteenth century Russia, and among South American Indians and peoples of the Caribbean. Indeed, the first thing the Nazis did in their death camps was to shave the heads of their prisoners, robbing them of adornment, identity, and power. Military recruits most likely are subjected to complete buzz-cuts for similar reasons.

Sigmund Freud (surprise, surprise) thought the head was a phallic symbol and that hair represented semen. Baldness, then, became a symbol, in Freud's view, for impotence or castration. But it must be remembered that Doctor Freud developed his theory without the benefit of viewing Kojak reruns.

The Aryans depicted the sun, the giver of all life, as having long, flaming red hair. In the seventeenth century, when the persecution of witches was at its height in this country, it was believed that the power to bewitch lay especially in the hair. It was standard practice not only to shave witches' heads, but also to depilate their entire bodies, thus rendering them hairless and harmless before execution.

Hair, then, has always been thought of as an expression of life and strength, of individual and collective identity, and as a repository of magical and religious powers, for good and for evil. Hair has also been used in a number of cultures to maintain a relationship with the dead. Among the Iroquois a lock of hair from the dead was given to the nearest surviving relative. The Zuni believed that to burn the hair of a dead family member or friend, and then to inhale the smoke, produced good health for those left behind. In this country in the eighteenth and nineteenth centuries jewelry was often made from the hair of the dearly departed. This attachment to the dead through their hair may owe to the fact that the hair of the deceased may continue to grow for a time. Life may flee the heart, but it ebbs from the hair.

The last two decades in this country have witnessed a backlash from the bald. Balding men in America more often see hair as an all or nothing proposition, where many choose the latter, minimalist option. Female opinions on the bald look, however, decidedly seem parted in the middle. If I were losing my hair, I think I might go for the bald look. Some of the men I admire most had little or no hair: Julius Caesar, Aristotle, and Popeye, to name a few. There is a kind of defiance in the bald look, but this "King and I" scorched earth policy requires more courage and confidence than I think I could muster. The last time I had little or no hair was in high school. In my graduation picture my ears stuck out of the sides of my head like the wide-open front doors of a 1952 Buick sedan.

I think I would go with the flip.

THE CARE-TAKER MONKEYS

Anything which can be made funny must have
at its heart some tragic implications.
Karl Menninger
A Psychiatrist's World

In all kinds of activity it is important to know
how to stop before what you do not know ruins
what you do know.
Leo Tolstoy
Last Diaries

Long ago in the northwest of India, by the river Ganges, there lived a rich and noble king, a member of the exalted Kshatriya clan, a descendant of the Indo-Aryan invaders. The king was the possessor of great amounts of land that included an enormous palace, extraordinary stables with the most beautiful horses in all of India, and an impressive park, complete with its own zoo full of exotic animals from around the world.

One day the king's park-keeper asked permission from the king to attend a religious festival in a city many miles away, near the river Indus. Many of the other workers in the park already had left for the festival, one of the most important and impressive of the year, and the park-keeper did not want to miss it.

The king reluctantly gave his permission, but with the stipulation that the park-keeper first must find someone reliable to water the trees. It seems that the king, at great expense to himself and the citizens of the kingdom, had brought an amazing variety of trees to his kingdom, and was quite proud of their beauty and wondrous variation. As he had with the animals in his zoo, the king gathered flora from the four corners of the earth, in much the way the Macedonian king, Alexander the Great, had returned from his conquests with specimens for his zoo-keeper, Aristotle.

But finding someone to water and care for the trees was not an easy matter. The park-keeper searched throughout the park for someone to help him with the trees, but it was late in the day, and all the other workers themselves had gone to the festival. Indeed, as he reached the eastern edge of the park, off in the distance he could see the bright colors of the park workers garments receding in the distance. He could hear the fading music of the flutes the workers played to pass the time on their long journey.

Given the king's fondness for his trees, this was clearly a matter that his royal highness would not wish left undone, so the park-keeper continued to search throughout the park for someone who might help him in the care of the trees. But after thoroughly searching the entire park, he could find no one to help but a band of monkeys that regularly congregated in the western end of the park, near the zoo. Reluctantly, the park-keeper summoned the chief of the monkeys. The chief was a monkey who had always prided himself on his great wisdom and decisiveness. Indeed, the other monkeys were greatly impressed by the chief's great vocabulary. When the monkeys had their meetings in an abandoned cave on the edge of the kingdom, the chief frequently would talk for hours, the other monkeys often wondering what quite a few of the words meant. All the monkeys were in clear agreement, however, that the chief was the most impressive leader they possibly could have.

"Is it possible that you and the other monkeys might water the trees for me during my leave?" the park-keeper asked. "The king is very concerned about the matter, and you know how the king can be. He is very particular about his trees. This is not a matter about which we could safely make a mistake."

And so, the chief of the monkeys, responding in quite a rhetorical flourish of his own, promised to see to the watering. The park-keeper, having left the necessary water pots, and now knowing first hand of the chief of the monkeys extensive vocabulary, confidently went off to his festival in the city by the river Indus.

When the time came for the watering of the trees the chief monkey said to the other monkeys who had gathered to take up the watering pots, "One moment please, this is very serious business, it clearly involves the gravest of matters, the park-keeper is very concerned, indeed, dare I say 'adamant' that we do a good job. The king has brought this foliage from prodigious distances, he has made an extraordinary outlay of funds, so we also must use the water economically so as not to have the king incur undo further financial encumbrances. How might we accomplish these tasks? The nourishment of the trees, as well as the imperative for fiscal restraint and responsibility? I leave it to you my faithful servants to suggest ways we might proceed."

At first all the other monkeys looked at each other with blank stares. Some looked at the ground, while others shifted back and forth on one leg and then the other. For several moments no one spoke. Some thought to themselves, "The chief is the one with the big vocabulary, why doesn't he figure it out?"

Finally, one of the braver monkeys suggested a plan.

"We must water the trees according to their needs," the reticent monkey said.

"But how can we know what their needs might be?" another monkey asked inquisitively.

For the longest time, all the monkeys stared at their chief, or at the ground.

"The trees with the longest roots need the most water, and trees with the shortest roots need the least," the chief finally said. "This is an elementary deduction for one with such a vocabulary as mine."

And so the chief of the monkeys went on to organize the labor by dividing the monkeys into teams of two, using his impressive vocabulary at every step of the way. The strongest monkey in each pair was told to pull up a tree from the ground to see if it has long or short roots. The other monkey of each pair carried the water pot.

"This is a complicated matter having both biologic and economic ramifications. But I, your chief, have devised a plan," the chief continued to say.

"If the tree has short roots," the monkey chief said confidently, "then you should water it less. And if it has long roots, why then you should water it more." And so the monkeys divided their labor in this way. They watered each of the beautiful and expensive trees in the garden. In a very short time, in the midst of the chief's great vocabulary and the worker monkeys' great diligence, all the trees died.

LACROSSE

*Lacrosse is a simple game played by
complicated people in a web of
Byzantine social relations.*
Anonymous Johns Hopkins University Lax All-American

Lacrosse. For most of the nation's inhabitants, "La Crosse" is a city in southwestern Wisconsin, but for a certain segment of Baltimore's population lacrosse is a century old way of life. At its best this way of life disdains the big money of sports. At its worst, lacrosse has been a symbol of a Baltimore privileged class, with complicated rules about who does and does not get to play the game.

To the outsider, lacrosse is a curious game. In the national imagination it is something akin to curling or ice bowling. It has a French name, was invented by Native Americans, and, until quite recently, was played mostly by up-state New York Indians with missing front teeth in empty ice hockey rinks and by white Baltimore boys from prep schools in the northern part of the city.

Lacrosse is most likely the oldest of American team sports. It was played by the Six Nations of the Iroquois throughout northern New York and Canada long before Christopher Columbus landed in what he thought was the New World. The Hurons and Algonquins called the game *baggataway*. They often played with as many as a thousand participants on a side, and with goals ten miles apart. Their contests started at dawn and lasted until sundown, or until one side gave up or ran out of warriors who could still stand.

The Native Americans saw lacrosse as a good preparation for war. In Baltimore, since the turn of the century, lacrosse has been seen as character development for the corporate wars. It has been a game played by boys who often went off to Princeton or stayed home to play at Johns Hopkins, a school, at least when it came to lacrosse, with a curious combination of the mystique of Knute Rockne's Notre Dame football teams, the 1927 Yankees, and the invincibility of Bruno Samartino in his wrestling heyday.

For most of its American history lacrosse has been one of the games of choice of privileged Baltimoreans, but in the last quarter century it has undergone a movement toward egalitarianism. It has spread across the country and down the social ladder, with missionary haves bringing it to the have-nots. Philanthropic organizations like the Abel Foundation have established teams and clinics in the inner-city. It is played in nearly every Baltimore high school, public and private, in the greater Baltimore area. There are rec teams, girls' teams, club teams, women's teams, and professional box lacrosse teams, but it still remains a sport where a stick costs three times more than a baseball glove and five times more than a basketball.

But lacrosse should not be reduced to sociology, any more than Nuryev could be summed up with the tools of Newtonian physics. Lacrosse is a game with uncommon grace and symmetry. It is a game with an inner beauty rarely matched by other American team sports. It has the cerebral strategy of baseball, without the down time. It has the brute force of football, but not the gratuitous violence. It combines the passing of ice hockey, the acrobatics and fast breaks of basketball, and the cleverness of a well-played game of chess.

Lacrosse is played by people who look like normal human beings, not the steroid produced refrigerator-size anomalies of football, or even many of the professional baseball players of our day. It is a game where no one makes a million dollars, unless it's selling stocks after they have been All-Americans at Hopkins.

If one is to find the soul of the game of lacrosse—the most American of sports—it is that it always has held to a salvation by works, not by grace. It is a game where the team who works the hardest usually wins. It is a game where showing up, doing your job the right way, and not making any glaring mistakes usually brings success. Some are good at the game because they have played it a long time. They often were born with silver spoons in their mouths and lacrosse sticks in their cribs. Others, often more gifted athletes, pick up the game quickly, making a mark on the sport in a remarkably short time.

However one comes to the game, winning does not come without very hard work. Indeed, the greatest player to ever play the game was an African-American who with natural gifts and an uncanny ability to do more than anyone else on the field later made a fairly good career in another sport. This man scored five goals by half-time of the 1957 college All-Star game. His name is Jim Brown.

Chapter 3

So Deeply Into Suffering

The Best of All Possible Worlds

With this pitiful earthly Euclidean understanding
all I know is that there is suffering and that there
are some who are not guilty; that cause follows
effect simply and directly; that everything flows
and finds its own level—but that's only Euclidean nonsense.

Fyodor Dostoyevsky
The Brothers Karamazov

All Nature is but Art, unknown to thee;
All Chance, Direction, which thou canst not see;
All Discord, Harmony not understood;
All partial Evil, Universal Good;
And spite of Pride, in erring Reason's spite,
One truth is clear, whatever is, is right.

Alexander Pope
An Essay on Man

From its beginnings, Gottfried Wilhelm Leibniz's life was an unusual one. His father, an esteemed professor of moral philosophy at the University of Leibzig, might have been an important influence on his son's philosophical and spiritual development had he not died when the young Leibniz was just celebrating his sixth birthday. Although Leibniz was essentially self-taught (he had learned algebra by four, and by eight he had mastered Greek and Latin well enough to be doing his own translations of Thucydides and Plato, Marcus Aurelius and Seneca), he did not learn those few important things that only come with a proper relationship with a good father.

The same day he received his Ph.D. from Altdorf in 1666, Leibniz was offered a professorship at the university, an extraordinary feat in any age. A short time later, under the sponsorship of the Elector of Mainz, Leibniz entered a life of public service, which included a noble attempt at reconciling the Roman church with the Protestant faiths in the German speaking world. He refused an invitation to head the Vatican Library, and, in the same year, Leibniz was the only Prussian ever elected to the Royal Society of London.

In his spare time, Leibniz visited Spinoza in Holland when others thought the Jewish scholar a pariah; he unsuccessfully attempted to convince Louis XIV that the muscle of the French army might be better put to use on the Egyptians than the Dutch; he founded the Berlin Academy of Sciences; he invented a mechanical calculator that in addition to simple arithmetic functions also could extract square roots; and, independently of Sir Isaac Newton, Leibniz discovered integral and differential calculus.

But by the end of G.W. Leibniz's illustrious life the discovery of calculus had proven to be more heartache than earlier he could have imagined. The followers of Newton, jealous and protective of their mentor's reputation, branded the Prussian philosopher a plagiarist, even though the two calculaic notations were so vastly different there could have been no borrowing one way or the other.

Shortly before these unsavory accusations against Leibniz were made, the Queen of Prussia consulted with the philosopher about a philosophical problem that apparently had left the young Queen sleepless. If God were all good, all knowing, and all powerful, the Queen wished to know, then why was there so much suffering in the world?

For the next thirteen years, in obedient service to the insomniac queen, Leibniz labored on this theological conundrum. His *Essays on Theodicy* was the fruit of those labors. In this book, Leibniz pondered the nature and attributes of God, the problem of God's omniscience and human freedom, and the theological issue of suffering. In his *Essays on Theodicy*, Leibniz boldly put forth the theory that all that happens in this life works toward the good. By the second decade of the eighteenth century, *Essays on Theodicy* had become the standard philosophical text on these matters. The book was translated into dozens of languages, and regularly referred to in both Catholic and Protestant pulpits all over the Europe of the Enlightenment.

Ironically, Leibniz's life had been hitherto untouched by the more practical aspects of suffering. He had lived essentially disconnected from the world and its troubles. He had lived, more or less, unacquainted with the world, protected by favorable conditions. Leibniz was able to commit himself to the life of the mind without the nagging distractions of illness or the doubts about one's reputation that often come for lesser scholars.

But then, at the end of Leibniz's life, the allegations of plagiarism surfaced. The rumors and subsequent charges and counter-charges plunged the Prussian philosopher into the kind of misery about which, heretofore, he had only written in a theoretical way. He was convinced of his innocence, and yet, very few others were. It was not merely a question of misfortune, but also one of a heavy burden of blame that attached itself to him, no matter how blameless he knew himself to be. Indeed, while thousands of carriages lined up around London to enter Highgate Cemetery for Newton's funeral, only two carriages, one filled with grave diggers, accompanied Leibniz to his final resting place.

At the end of his life Leibniz was intellectually and spiritually wounded. And there awakened in his soul a doubt about whether these unsavory events could indeed be part of all that works for the good. In a reflective man like Leibniz such doubts often take deep root. He began to wonder about whether God is love. And this and other like questions began to have more and more power over the imagination of Leibniz. One could say that the problem of innocent suffering became, first, a practical reality for him, and then, in later life when enough sand had moved through the hourglass, an obsession.

In the throes of his greatest despair, Leibniz, while on a fitful holiday in Italy, met an older Italian priest on the streets of Rome. It was in Saint Peter's Square. A pigeon had landed on the old priest's head, and the great philosopher took this as a sign: perhaps, after all, God was directing all things for the good.

In veiled terms, the philosopher opened his heart to the old cleric. Leibniz spoke of a great tragedy that had befallen him. He falsely had been accused in a manner that had called into question his reputation, the very core of his being. The accusations also brought into doubt his intellectual gifts, as well as his moral character. His was a highly specialized field. There were brilliant men at odds with each other. The entire matter had left him feeling vulnerable, spent, and angry—especially at God.

The priest listened intently for several hours. In that time, he began to understand both the philosopher's sorrow and his immense intelligence and sensitivity. Indeed, the priest fancied himself as a man who kept abreast of the times. He considered himself a thinker of sorts. And so, the old priest set out to prove to his anonymous German traveler that these troubles of his would all, in the end, work toward the good. "If God is love, and if this is the best of all possible worlds, then all things must work for the good," the priest said.

But after a few hours of conversation it became clear to the old cleric that the German's intellect far surpassed his own. In fact, the German seemed to have a well phrased criticism ready at every crucial point in the old priest's argument. Finally, after several attempts at overcoming the philosophers' objections, the priest threw up his hands and said to Leibniz: "It would seem that I have but one counsel left to give you. There is a book about the love of God and the nature of suffering I wish to give you. It is a wise book, and is written by one of your countrymen. If this book is no service to you, then I fear no one can help you with your despair. It is called *Essays on Theodicy* and is written by the distinguished philosopher G.W. Leibniz.

THE SMILING RABBI

Now Sarah said, "God has brought laughter
for me; and everyone who hears will laugh with me."
Genesis 21:6

We do not completely love those at whom we cannot smile.
Andre Maurois
The Art of Living

The morning the rabbi died the sky was a pewter color, with oddly bright shafts of sunlight, the size and shape of glistening steel girders, periodically breaking through the gray. For an instant wide beams of light would penetrate the death camp until a moment later ashen clouds drifted in and smothered the light.

Rabbi Izak had been in the camp for three years, an unusually long time for an old man to last. In that time he had done hard labor, digging trenches and constructing wooden bunk houses. But it was now his turn to die. At dawn he joined the serpentine queue waiting to be admitted to the gas chamber. The line was uneven, fat in the middle and thin on the ends, as if it were a snake that had swallowed something whole.

At first the rabbi stood silently, naked and unashamed. All around him in small knots of humanity unclad prisoners embraced. Others prayed, quietly and alone. Some old men had fallen to the ground and were beating it with their fists until guards came forward with dogs to keep the line moving. Two guards a piece grabbed them under the arms and frog walked the wailing men to the death waiting at the front of the line. Some squeezed fists full of dark earth as they were dragged forward, their naked heels digging into the cold, dark earth.

When one of the fierce rays of sunlight periodically broke through the gray sky, Rabbi Izak squinted for a moment, perhaps surprised and blinded by the light. But in the next instant he began to smile. It was more like a grin, really. At first it spread tentatively across his dry, cracked lips. Then it became more defined, settling in his eyes as if suddenly he had remembered something the guards did not know.

For the next few hours the line slowly grew shorter. The wailing men, and the embracing women, those who nakedly prayed for a miracle or simply for forgiveness, and the thin teen age girls worried about their exposed breasts, they all were gone, their bodies transported from the back of the gas chamber to the waiting crematoria by skinny prison workers in ill-fitting striped uniforms. By ten o'clock Rabbi Izak was near the front of the queue. And through it all, the naked holy man kept the knowing smile on his lips.

Around 10:30 the commandant left his office and was on his way home to let out the family dog. The commandant's wife usually took care of the pets, but today, after dropping the children off at the camp school she had decided to go into town to see about reupholstering a sofa that sat in the family's parlor. They had received the dog six months before, as a house-warming present when they arrived at the camp. But the puppy, a shepherd, was high strung and had managed to chew off a good portion of the facing of the couch, so that the white stuffing now was showing through. Late the previous evening, after their children had gone to bed, the commandant and his wife while sitting up in bed had argued about the dog. For the first time in their long marriage, they had broken their rule about never falling asleep angry with each other.

The commandant did not normally walk home by way of the gas chamber and the crematoria. But it had rained the evening before and the hill leading up to his house was muddy and beginning to erode. He was wearing a pair of new boots that had just been sent from Berlin, so he walked the long way around trying to avoid the mud, past the queue where the rabbi waited, grinning and unbowed.

At first the commandant paid little attention to the line of prisoners. Shortly after becoming the head of the camp he had made a conscious, and some thought curious, decision to spend most of his time on the administrative aspects of the job. His presence was rarely felt in the "yard." Some of his subordinates said he did not have what it takes to run a large camp. After a month or so, he had found the more hands-on features of the camp were best left to others with a taste for such things. He had decided, after discussing it with a trusted friend, that he would let his subordinates say what they wished, but he was not the sort of man who could get too close to such matters.

At first, the commander paid little attention to the remaining thirty or so prisoners lined up in twos at the metal gas chamber door. All but the rabbi were wailing and gnashing their teeth. Something welled up in the commander when his eyes met those of the gaunt and smiling rabbi. "Find out what is wrong with that man," the commandant said crisply to the sergeant who had been organizing the morning's exterminations and the subsequent disposal of the dead. Izak swayed side by side as if listening to music no one else could hear.

The sergeant, a large man with a stammer, had known Rabbi Izak from the beginning. They had arrived at the camp on the same day. The sergeant was then a corporal and his job had been to separate prisoners from their luggage upon arrival. The sergeant remembered that three years before, the rabbi had handed the young corporal his yalmuke, while making a joke in Yiddish the younger man did not understand.

Now the old rabbi shuffled slowly toward the great iron door of the gas chamber. From the front of the queue the sergeant shouted at the old man to stop. The grinning rabbi immediately halted, his eyes fixed on the charcoal horizon, his gaunt, yellow body swaying ever so slightly. The sergeant mumbled something to the rabbi, and a moment later the subordinate returned to the waiting officer, saying that Rabbi Izak had refused to speak.

The commandant's face became flushed, and he muttered something in a Bavarian accent that those around him did not quite hear. He approached the rabbi, moving within a foot of the old man's face. "What is wrong with you?" the commandant repeated. Rabbi Izak stopped his swaying and stared straight ahead, as if focusing on something above and to the right of his interrogator's head. But through these moments the grin held steadily on old man's face, a white light reflected in his deep blue eyes, while those prisoners

49

around him stopped their wailing long enough to listen and to watch the rabbi and the commandant.

"I said, 'What is wrong with you?'" the commandant repeated loudly, tilting his head slightly to the right, a small piece of his spittle inadvertently striking the rabbi's cheek.

There was a long silence while the rabbi again stared at the horizon. Finally the old man's glistening eyes for the first time met the blue irises of the commander's. "There is nothing wrong with me," the rabbi said softly. "But perhaps there is something wrong with you. You have the curious idea that you have control over my life, and thus you wish to frighten me, even in my last moments. But there is something amusing in this. Only God controls my life—and He controls today what I might make of my own death. This morning I am certain Yashem wishes me to smile." And the rabbi again began to sway ever so slightly, the gray clouds swirling above them all, the grin again appearing on his thin lips.

There was another long silence in the air as the commandant looked at his new boots. Then he slowly walked behind the old man. A moment later the commander's pistol broke the silence, the bullet entering the back of the rabbi's skull. The old man died instantly, the grin still fixed on his face, drops of bright red blood falling on the commandant's black boots.

In another instant a wide shaft of light penetrated the muddy yard of the camp. Then it seemed to move along the train tracks for an instant, until it veered off and spread out into the fallow wheat field just on the other side of the fence. But a moment later the light was swallowed by heavy, drifting clouds. The leaden clouds swirled and mingled for a while, everything was again eerily silent, and then it began to rain.

Supremum Vale[*]

Naturam expelles furca tamen usque recurret.
You may drive nature out with a fork, but it will still return.

Horace
The Epistles

The remission of sins, for it is by this that the
church on earth stands: it is through this that
what has been lost, and was found, is saved
from being lost again.

Augustine
Enchiridion

When Samuel Purchase entered the old priest's hospital room, the first thing he noticed were the cleric's hands. They were chapped and red and battered from the comings and goings of too many nurses and too many IVs. As he stared at the bony hand resting on the edge of the bed, Purchase was surprised at how small it looked. Then the younger man became transfixed by one of the prominent veins that had collapsed, leaving a small, purple cruciform bruise on the back of the priest's right hand. Purchase remembered the Thanksgiving dinner thirty-five years before when, as a ten year old boy, while passing the mash potatoes, he thought about stabbing the priest with a dinner fork in the back of that same hand.

A few months before that dinner, in the heat of summer, the priest had taken the young Samuel Purchase camping. It was in the cool of the evening the first day of the trip in an old army surplus, olive drab tent, with summer cicada humming in the grass just on the other side of the canvas wall, that the priest molested the boy.

While it was happening, the young Purchase thought about the priest's hands raised above his head during the consecration. From his vantage point of a knelling altar boy, the priest's uplifted hands and the wafer they held seemed small and distant. A moment later he thought about that part of the mass, before the consecration, when the altar boy carried two small cruets containing oil and water, so that the priest could anoint and then wash his fingers. Afterwards, the priest would dry his hands and drape the starched linen finger towel over the waiting arm of the altar boy.

During the violation, just before the priest had finished, there was a ringing in the boy's ears, like the sound of the Good Humor truck or the bells of the consecration. A few weeks after the camping trip, when Purchase somehow found the courage to tell his parents about what had happened in the tent, they did not believe him.

For the next eight years, through the remainder of grade school and high school, the boy lived silently with a fear that it all had been a dream, perhaps some sort of optical illusion like the forgiveness of sins, or the changing of bread and wine into the body and blood of Christ. In these years, the boy had regular contact with the priest: bowling, pizza, family dinners; but nothing was ever said about the violation.

Except for that brief moment when he, with fork in hand, paused over the mash potatoes and thought about stabbing the priest in the back of the hand, Samuel Purchase had done little outwardly to indicate the depth or the intensity of his feelings about that summer night.

When he was eighteen years old, however, Purchase confronted the priest in the confessional. For two hours in line Samuel Purchase had waited patiently—behind several old women with black rosaries wrapped around their folded hands, and a bent-up rail of a man with a rough cough—for his turn in the box.

Finally, through the iron-work of the confessional box opening, the young Purchase could see the priest's right hand resting on the edge of the wooden ledge that separated them. A small dim bulb, like a child's night light, shown just above and to the left of the priest's head. In a slow, thin voice the boy confessed a litany of venial sins, and, in the end, almost as an addendum to the confession, he found some courage in a secret room in the back of his soul that he thought had been sealed shut the day he tried to tell his parents about the priest.

"Why did you lie about hurting me?" the young man heard himself say.

In the dimness of the confessional the boy could see the priest lift his hand from the ledge and wipe something invisible from the side of his face.

"I don't know what you are talking about," the priest whispered. "Small boys have a way of making up fantastic stories...Perhaps you have imagined it...Do you still wish to have absolution?"

For a moment there was a silence between them, like the interval between the sight of lightning and the crashing sound made by the thunder that follows it. Young Samuel Purchase left the confessional before the priest had finished the absolution, and so he knew nothing of the nature of his penance; nor did he return to that church ever again.

Now, twenty-seven years later, Samuel Purchase looked out the double-paned window of the hospital room, as the day's remaining light collected on the horizon. The color of the sunset appeared as though there might be some great fire on the other side of the world, and the yellow, burnt orange, and violet line on the edge of the earth was the only sign of the conflagration.

Purchase sat next to the priest who had fallen asleep before the younger man's arrival. He had not called before hand. The young man thought the priest might refuse to see him. Purchase examined the sleeping cleric's hand, the purple bruise standing out like a cross on the back of a priest's Easter vestments. The younger man looked to the tray of partially eaten food next to the bed. Two pieces of dried turkey, a few morsels of lumpy potatoes, and a dab of what looked to be cranberry sauce remained on the plate, along with a white plastic knife and fork. The knife remained in its plastic wrapper.

For a moment, something familiar and strange welled up in the younger man. He stared at the fork, and then at the dying man and began to name it. But a moment later, the priest's eyes flickered, and immediately he was aware of Samuel Purchase's presence in the room.

"I wanted to come before it was too late," Samuel Purchase said.

The young man paused. Then he breathed deeply, as if he might find courage in the air. "You know it is customary in our tradition to be given absolution only after a full confession."

Samuel Purchase took another deep breath that felt something like inhaling a forgotten part of his soul, his eyes remained fixed on the rhythmic rising and falling of the old man's chest.

"I understand why you lied, and I wanted you to know before you die," the young man said, "that I want you to die in peace."

The old man's bony head turned slightly to the right and their eyes met, for the briefest of moments, for the first time in thirty-five years.

"We both need to complete this confession," Samuel Purchase whispered. "I need to know you are sorry. I need to know you remember the truth...I have to have some sort of sign."

For a long moment the old priest did not move. Then his right hand slowly lifted off the edge of the bed, paused, suspended for another moment, and then finally met the younger man's grasp. The old man squeezed with what little strength he could find. This simple act drained from the priest what small bit of energy remained in his broken body. Tears welled in the old man's yellowed eyes.

Samuel Purchase again looked out the window to discover the lights of the hospital's parking garage flickering on. A moment later he heard an announcement made over the public address system: "Dr. Thomas, Dr. Thomas...1746..." And then the jangled crash of what sounded like silverware hitting the hallway floor. Purchase stood for a moment beside the bed, perhaps expecting something more to happen, as the older man's face turned toward the wall.

"Supremum vale," the younger man whispered, "absalvo tue." And he left the room.

(Supreme vale *can be translated in a number of ways. Supreme is an adjective that can be translated as "last," "final," "ultimate," and "definitive." The noun* vale *can be translated as "farewell" and "goodbye."*)

NEMESIS LAME

*Nemesis is lame, but she is often of colossal
stature; and sometimes while her sword is
not yet unsheathed, she stretches out her
huge left arm and grasps her victim. The
mighty hand is invisible, but the victim totters
under the dire clutch, nevertheless.*

George Eliot
Letters

*We must assume our existence as broadly as we
in any way can; everything, even the unheard of,
must be possible in it. That is, at bottom the only
courage that is demanded of us; to have courage
for the most extraordinary, the most singular and
the most inexplicable that we may encounter.*

Rainer Maria Rilke
Letters to a Young Poet

A s the man opened the envelope containing the request, he paused
for the briefest of moments, the way a surgeon might stand poised,
shiny-sharp scalpel in hand, for an instant above an anesthetized
patient before making an important incision. The man had not
known Phillip all that well. They grew up in the same working class
part of town, but they had not known each other as children. The
man, following that complicated collection of hedgerows and cul-de-
sacs that fate had laid out for him, was now a professor. Phillip had
escaped as well, becoming an attorney after leaving the state university's law school. Both men had been scholarship students, and it was

the feeling of being an impostor that forged their periodic social bond.

The two had met more than two decades before; they saw each other at parties, and talked about the old neighborhood. The professor remembered that most of their conversations had been about time, and how this invisible agent had changed them and the neighborhood. But time meant little now. Phillip had died the day before and thus already he had passed into that eternal state that the living reserve for the dead. It is a place where the dead stay frozen. They do not age. The expressions on their faces remain fixed. The dead, for their part, are so busy being frozen they can do nothing else. It becomes a full-time job. As the professor's graduate school mentor had once said, "The dead are not very good friends. They don't call, they don't write. We make the dead frozen and then they ignore us."

The man figured the letter he held in his hands must have been written the day before Phillip's death. He stared at the neat, black handwriting, thinking that perhaps he would find something peculiar in words from the grave. Instead it was the request he found odd. It sat on the page like a personal ad:

> I wonder if you would do me an enormous favor. You know, I have always loved your writing. It is rare, for it comes from the head and the heart. You seem to know, before it is too late, what it is about a life that might be important. I know you might find this an odd request, but would you give the homily at my funeral service?

The man turned the single piece of paper over in his hands. Phillip had died of AIDS. He had gathered that from the way the obituary, which he had read with his morning coffee, carefully had been worded. Now, holding the letter in the privacy of his study, the professor's first thought was a secret one, a reflexive one, like pupils reacting to sudden light. If he were to honor the request, he thought, might others mistakenly think he too was gay? Perhaps they would think he and Phillip had been lovers.

Later, in the evening, he thought about how the most difficult part of being a Pharisee is trying to deny it to oneself. But in the morning, after a night of restless sleep, the professor's thoughts looked something more like courage. He would do the homily, and tell what he knew of the humor and gentleness of this man with whom he shared a vanishing neighborhood.

For the next two days, the man worked in his study on the homily. October light poured through the open windows, while scarlet leaves, in ones and twos, gave up their hold on life. In the mail, on the third day, a letter came from a suburban priest with directions to the church. And with it came the enclosure—a tribute to the fallen Phillip—written for the pale green weekly church bulletin by the pastor.

The professor scanned the tribute. It spoke of Phillip's life of service; his career with the government; his interest in sports; and his sustained involvement in various charities. And then, at the end, was the paragraph:

"Jesus embraced people of all life-styles. He loved the sinner but hated the sin. We must remember, in our hour of grief—God loves Phillip anyway."

When the man arrived at the church, it was nearly filled. Straight shafts of fierce golden light poured into the pews and the sanctuary. The priest introduced himself, and said that he was looking forward to the professor's comments. He hoped the professor could stay for lunch.

The gospel reading was about good trees bearing bad fruit. The man's prepared remarks had followed rather closely with the movement of the gospel story. He had kept in mind Phillip's note about the importance of writing from the head and the heart.

After he read the gospel, the priest introduced the man as a "dear friend of Phillip's." The professor straightened his tie. For an instant, he thought of it as perhaps the modern equivalent of Job girding his loins. Then, in the next moment, he looked out on the first few rows of the congregation. Most of those gathered there held the pale green church bulletins up to shield their eyes from the fierce light. And almost against his will, the man wondered if they thought he was Phillip's lover.

When he approached the podium the man drew his prepared remarks from his breast pocket, a half smile invented on his tense face. But a moment later, he pressed the six page homily into a neat fold and returned it to his jacket. Then he leaned out over the front of the podium, the way a nervous man might watch a precious object he just now inadvertently dropped fall from a great height.

The man paused again, cleared his throat, and met the eyes of a few parishioners in the back pews where the light had not yet reached. Finally, he spoke in a soft and clear voice, "If you have never been embarrassed or disappointed by any of the particulars of your sexual life—by thoughts or deeds—I would like you to stand up now."

At first, there was an eerie silence. Then there was a flutter in the church that sounded like the beating of a single pair of great wings. A breeze had folded back the sanctuary curtains. Members of the congregation looked left and right, the brilliant autumn light still filtering through the stain-glass windows. Some still held the pale green church bulletins up to their faces to shield themselves from the glare. For the next several moments, people murmured and squinted, but no one rose. Then the professor took another long, slow breath, the way a man might who was trying to rid himself of the hiccups.

"Ought Jesus to love us, anyway?" he heard himself say.

And he sat down amidst the stark light pouring into the sanctuary, and prepared himself for the consecration.

THE CLERK'S IMMORTALITY

When a man is wrapped up in himself,
it usually makes a pretty small package.

John Ruskin

Essays

And how little to have gained from the
experience of life, if one's thoughts are
lingering still upon personal fulfillments,
and not rooted in the knowledge that the
great immortalities, Love, Goodness,
and Truth, include all others; and one need
pray for no lesser survivals.

Alice James

Diary

In a kingdom not so long ago nor so far away there lived a great and noble sovereign. The king was wise and kind, not to mention quite philosophical, something unusual for a king in this or any other land save the Republic of Plato. It was his habit to take long rides across the length and breadth of his kingdom, usually accompanied by his many viziers.

One day, in the company of his viziers, the king stopped atop a mountain so that the horses might rest. The king sat up straight in his saddle and surveyed his lands spread out before them. His holdings were many, his people were prospering, and the kingdom was at peace for the first time in many years. The wise monarch felt the kind of secret pride that only comes with being a noble and just king.

As the king's eyes moved across the landscape toward the windward side of the mountain, he was reminded that summer was coming to a close and that autumn would soon be upon them. Then, a moment later, a terrible thought welled up in the noble king. The thought sat uncomfortably in the king's philosophical heart, it was as if the gods had voted to forgo autumn immediately in favor of the coldest of winters.

"One day I will die, and in my dying I will leave all this," the king mournfully declared.

The king's viziers, as if in one voice, echoed the sovereign's lament. "Yes, your Highness, death is a cruel and unspeakable horror. It is the worm at the core of all our pretension to happiness," as each thought about what he would lose—family, wealth, and honor. But one of the viziers, on a rather unimpressive dappled horse, remained silent through all these laments.

"I wish we could live forever," the king exclaimed. "It is a cruel trick that immortality is reserved only for the gods." And again his nobles sadly nodded in agreement, but the silent vizier on the dappled horse now began to chuckle softly.

The king continued his lament. "Think of all the hunting and feasts, the drama and music, the affairs of the heart we all have enjoyed. If we were immortal, these pleasures of life would never end. We would never worry about growing old, we would never see sickness or grieve, nor would we ever succumb to all the sufferings the gods have planned for us."

And through it all the viziers nodded their rueful assent—all but the chuckling vizier on the small dappled horse. But now, in these few moments, his chuckle had turned to a genuine laugh.

"To live forever, as we are now in the prime of life," said the king, who now began to keep one curious eye on the laughing vizier. "An eternity of happiness, what more could we wish for from the gods?"

The lords again nodded, murmuring approval, but the laughing vizier continued in his mirth to the point that the king stopped his lament in mid-sentence, examining the man on the dappled horse. "What is it that you find so amusing?" the sovereign inquired testily. "I see nothing at all comical about the subject at hand. Death is a sorrowful thing. Perhaps you have lost your senses and a good fifty lashes or so might restore them to you."

The laughing vizier bowed from astride his unimpressive dappled horse. "I do not mean to offend you Sire, nor would I much desire a taste of the whip. But I have been thinking of what your kingdom would be like if all of us gathered here were to live forever, as you so eloquently have suggested we might."

The laughing man continued. "If we all were immortal, then the heroes of old still would be among us: the great king who first brought us to this land, and who brought us freedom from our oppressors; and the great lawgiver who established for us our system of? laws, perhaps one of the finest creations of all humankind; the great philosophers and poets of old, too, would still be among us. Is it not true that compared to them, we all would be peasants, fit only to plough the fields, living with bad teeth and no real dreams to speak of? And you, my dear and noble king, what would be your fate? Why you would no doubt be a clerk, living in one of the outer provinces, spending your days shuffling papers and worrying about how to pay your taxes."

The king stared at the vizier on the dappled horse, while all the other viziers held their breaths. Then the king burst into laughter. "You are a wise and brave soul, my friend. More importantly, you speak the truth." And the king turned to the others and said, "For encouraging me in my vanity, I penalize you and myself, two draughts each of our finest wine."

Then the king dismounted, the others immediately following suit, and the wise sovereign warmly embraced the laughing vizier. "As for you, my laughing friend," the monarch decreed, "from this day forward you will have a new job. No longer will you be the least of my viziers. Whenever I lament about the finitude of life, whenever I grumble about my own death, your sole task will be to cry out 'A clerk! A clerk!' and I will return to my senses."

Holding on to Coattails

*No faith is our own
that we have not already
arduously won.*
Haverlock Ellis
The Dance of Life

*It is in the darkness of night
that faith in light
is most admirable.*
Edmond Rostand
Chanticleer

It had rained all morning. Dusk was now settling over the camp. It was a January day, so the combination of drifting gray clouds and Winter in the northern Ukraine made the darkness descend early. The prisoners had just returned from working. Most tended to the fields just north of the camp; others—more favored prisoners—did inside work.

There had been persistent rumors for a month or so that the camp was to be closed. Along with the rumors came theories about what they would do with the prisoners. Some said they were to be killed *en masse*. Others said that those who remained able to work would be transferred to one of the larger camps.

It was around 3:30 when the announcement came over the loud speaker. The voice had a north German accent. "You are to report immediately to the exercise yard. Anyone who fails to report will be shot on sight." The message repeated many times.

Panic surged through the camp like electrical current. People pushed their ways through doors. Prisoners screamed the names of friends and family. In a panic-stricken stampede, the prisoners moved toward the exercise yard, elderly people falling to the wet ground. When they arrived at the yard, the prisoners found two long pits, about six feet deep and fifty yards long. They had been dug while the prisoners were out on their work details.

The amplified German voice blared across the sound system again. "The camp is to be closed. Only the most healthy workers will be spared. Those who are able to jump to the other side of the pits will be taken to Janowska, where they will continue to help the war effort."

Even under the best of conditions it would have been impossible to jump over the pits, which measured almost twenty-five feet from side to side.

Among the thousands of prisoners in the yard that day was a rabbi, Israel Feldman. He had been in the camp for two years. During that time, he had developed an unusual friendship with a younger man, Adam Blaustein, a free-thinking Jew with few religious sentiments and, in the last few months, a tendency toward the blackest kind of despair. Although Blaustein admired the rabbi, he thought that only a lunatic could keep his faith under such circumstances.

"Feldman, this is a ridiculous game, why don't we sit down in the pit and wait for the bullets? By jumping we give these sadists the added pleasure of watching us fail. Let us make our last act one of defiance."

"My friend, if we simply sit down, then whom would we be defying?" the rabbi responded. "If we sit, we do not give God a chance."

The two men by now had reached the edge of the pits, which were rapidly filling up with the tangled bodies of the dead. The old rabbi looked down at his feet, which were swollen and riddled with sores. Then he glanced at his young friend, a walking skeleton with piercing green eyes. A moment later, the rabbi closed his eyes and as his aching feet left the ground he murmured, "We are jumping."

When they opened their eyes, they found themselves on the other side of the pits.

"We made it, we made it!" Blaustein shouted. He continued to repeat it, as if convincing himself it were true. "Rabbi, because of you I am alive. There must be a God in heaven. But how is it possible? How could we have made this leap?"

"With Yashem, anything is possible my friend. I was holding on to the goodness of my ancestors," said Rabbi Feldman. "I held firmly to the coattails of my father, and his father, and his father. It is goodness that brought us to the other side of the pit. The real mystery, my friend, is how you made it over the pit. What is the secret that brought you over to the other side?"

"This is simple," said Blaustein. "I was holding on to you, rabbi."

*That dear octopus from whose tentacles
we never quite escape, nor in our inner most
hearts never quite wish to, family.*
Dodie Smith
Dear Octopus

Chapter 4

That Dear Octopus

FINDING THE CENTER

*He had that fine quality found only among
the best of teachers to be forever leading
while seeming to follow.*
William James
Talks to Teachers

S ometimes a single day comes along that somehow is successful in reminding a man just how far he has strayed from the real center of things. On these rare days serendipity or grace intervenes, eliminating the superfluous so that which is necessary might show through. A few days ago, I traveled with my five-year-old son to the home of some dear friends, a farm house built in the nineteenth century in the Shenandoah Valley. The husband is a rough and tumble looking man in his sixties, a farmer turned auctioneer; his wife a gentle nurse who does home care for the dying. Their daughter, a willowy architect who now lives and works in the city, was the instrument of grace who brought us here to learn something important.

I had spent the cacophony of Christmas back in the city with the boy. I had made that yearly mistake common to single fathers of buying the child far too many gifts for the holiday, spending money I did not have, spreading cheer that was hard to find. More than anything on Christmas morning I had willed myself to forget a poem of Auden's:

All sins are attempts to fill voids
with the wrong things.

A few days later, in the country, the mistakenness, the hopeless-
ness of it all gradually began to become clear. In a single snow-filled
day the boy met two ancient horses who use the small farm as a
retirement home; he watched the collective curiosity of a neighbor's
small herd of dairy cows who dropped by to see who the new boy
was; the boy took his first turn driving a tractor, and, when the
snow was too powdery for making snowmen, he slid down a steep
pasture hill on a green plastic trash can lid. All this, and a game of
Monopoly at the kitchen table, were orchestrated by the man and
his wife.

At every turn the man had stayed one step ahead of the boy, knowing at every moment what the boy needed and what would seem gratuitous or patronizing. The man seemed to know instinctively when
to give the child free reign on the tractor, and when to give necessary
instruction, or more. Later in the evening, at a simple dinner of
spaghetti and home-made bread, the man gently pressed the boy for
answers to simple questions about the day's activities, or sat silently
attentive while the child expounded on the finer points of a video
game the older man would never see.

Throughout the day, it became clearer to me that I too was learning. The country is never silent. There always is something going
on, even in winter—the sound of an iron bell clanging in the wind;
the bleating of a single goat in a snowy pasture; the wind whistling
through the holes of an old red barn. These sounds are separate,
distinct, full of a kind of clarity that does not exist back in the city.
The apprehension of beauty comes in solitary ways in the country
as well.

I have learned that a man may come in among the hills for a day
or two on his way elsewhere and be filled instantly to overflowing
with the beauty of a place and with the beauty and gentility of the
people who live there. Are those who live here after a while, blind to
the beauty? Or is it that after a while the beauty of a valley and its
people become such a part of the way things are that they are no
longer noticed? They become like a beautiful woman who need not
constantly check her reflection in the mirror for she knows her God-
given looks are as natural and fleeting as the steam that rises from the
bodies of two old horses on a cold winter morning.

At the end of the day, after the boy had wrestled with the old man in the living room, after he had eaten his New Year's cake and after bedtime stories, while the boy was being snuggled into a feathery bed, the last thing he told his father was that this had been one of the best days of his "entire life."

It had.

The Looking Glass

You go not till I set you up a glass
Where you may see the inmost parts of you.
William Shakespeare
Hamlet

A man is nothing but what he becomes
in the eyes of his father.
Sigmund Freud
Letters

When Jonathan Swift was an old and broken man he was taken by his family into a madhouse in Dublin, a hospital he had founded earlier in his very productive life, along with other noted citizens. During his woeful incarceration Swift is said to have neglected his hygiene and it is also said that he often stood before a particular small mirror in the madhouse library, and, while looking himself over he muttered, "Who is this poor old soul? Who is this unfortunate old wretch, and why is he always following me? Couldn't someone in authority escort him from the premises? Guards! Guards! I will not have this vagabond following me. Turn out the scoundrel."

One of the great ironies of this story is that Swift, the master impersonator, a man who regularly managed to become the person he was creating at the time—now he is Isaac Bickerstaff, a clairvoyant astrologer; now the urbane Cadenus; now the playful Presto, or the amazed Lemuel Gulliver, or the fiery-eyed patriot, M.B. Drapier—in old age seemed dumbfounded by the image of the elderly lunatic he had become. It is said that he often tried to sneak up on the mirror in the hope of catching the old beggar asleep, so that he could turn him out himself. One of the most important signs of his lunacy was his inability, or perhaps his unwillingness, to recognize himself in the mirror. At the time of Swift's death in 1745, Swift had not made the connection that the man in the mirror was finally to be turned out along with him.

In the same section of Dublin, at the same time, there lived another man, a widowed cobbler, and his young son. The son was like a mirror in which the father beheld himself. And for the son too the father acted as a kind of reflection of what the younger man surely one day would become. Indeed, the townspeople would often remark how much alike the two men were in so many ways. After finishing his schooling, the younger man set up a cobbler's bench right next to his father's in the narrow shop. The father had given his son new cobbler's tools as a graduation present. The two men became inseparable. They rarely left the tiny shop or their small flat above it.

Although it was clear to them that both men saw themselves principally as a reflection of the other, they never spoke of it. Their daily conversations were characterized by cheerful small talk, the kind that was useless in terms of its content, but might have been quite valuable for what, in small but important ways, it revealed about the men. They talked about the weather, their simple likes and dislikes, and the characters of their customers, one never straying too far from the opinion of the other.

There were occasions, however, when the father would stop work at his bench and stand before his son's work space just a few feet away. The father would stand quietly for a moment examining his son, a sorrowful look on the older man's face, as if a marooned man were looking into a dark night sky in order to find his way. Finally, the older man would speak from the heaviness of his heart.

"My poor son, I can see you are falling into a quiet despair, and I don't know what I can do for you. Perhaps the work here is too much for the both of us. We could give it up, find a small cottage in the country. Perhaps we might find a new way for the both of us."

The father was always solicitous toward the son. And the older cobbler's observations about his son were always on the mark. But there was still a great unstated confusion between the two. You see, the father believed he was to blame for the son's deep melancholy, while the son harbored dark thoughts that after the death of his mother the son's life had been a series of occasions of great sorrow for his father. Despite this great confusion, this complicated knot that tied the two strings of their lives together, neither ever spoke of it.

For years the two went on this way. And every now and then the father again would make the remark about the son's deep melancholy. The son would sadly smile and then feel all the more guilty about the matter. Indeed, it was not long after making one of these comments that the father died at his bench, his cobbler's hammer poised above a pair of a small child's shoes he had been mending.

At the funeral, the son surrounded the casket with flowers and pictures of his father as a younger man. For the next several years the business prospered in ways it had not when the father was alive. But always there was present in the younger cobbler's soul a deep sorrow about the loss, and a vexing question about the real role the father had played in his life. Indeed, after a while he began so cleverly to imitate his father's voice and mannerism that at times it seemed to some that the older man had returned from the grave.

On some days the son now sat at his father's bench. He used his father's worn cobbler's tools. He smoked the older man's tobacco in the father's favorite pipe. Sometimes he wore the father's work smock, and on quiet evenings, after the shop had closed, the young man imagined his father talking to him, "Ah, my poor son, I can see you are again falling into a great despair. Perhaps you are working too hard."

The young cobbler thought of his father as the only person who had ever understood him, and yet, he was now unsure about the situation, for after his mother's death the father was the only confidant the young man had ever had. His father's soul was the only other he ever had known.

A few years later, the son began to have darker questions about the relationship: was the son pretending to be the father, or, was the father pretending to be the son? He would sit at the old cobbler's bench, and then at the son's. On other days he wondered how many men really lived in the small flat above the cobbler's shop. Who was the real man in despair? And what was the cause of that despair? Had one of them lost himself in the other? It was at about this time that the young man painted over the half of the shop's sign that read: "...And Son, Cobblers."

It was not long after this that the man began to spend all his time, when he was not preoccupied with his duties at the shop, thinking about these matters. But through it all the shop continued to turn an impressive profit. But the man was not at all sure who should receive the credit for the transformation.

After a while, it was not clear to the man whether his father had ever really known him at all. On other days, he stormed around the tiny shop, his pipe in hand, thinking perhaps his wife and son had never really existed.

At any rate, the son never married, and certainly he never understood the great irony of the relationship with his father—that the great confusion that existed between them would have been the same whether the father was living or dead. And it would have been no different, one suspects, if the son were to have died before his beloved father.

What we do know is the cobbler was eventually taken to the same madhouse as Jonathan Swift. He lived on the same wing as the madhouse library, but by then the mirror had been removed and Swift long had been moldering in his grave. The cobbler was said to have been a model patient. He enjoyed board games and a good pipe of tobacco in the evening after dinner.

THREE PIECES OF ADVICE

Knowledge can be communicated, but not wisdom.
Hermann Hesse
Siddhartha

This is what knowledge really is. It is finding
out something for oneself with pain, with joy,
with exultancy, with labor, and with all the
little ticking, breathing moments of our lives,
until it is ours as that only is ours which is
rooted in the structure of our lives.
Thomas Wolfe
The Web and the Rock

Long ago, in a far away kingdom, there lived a man who worked in an ancient library. The library was the greatest in the known world, and the man was the greatest of its librarians, and through hard work and diligence he also had become his kingdom's greatest scholar. But the librarian's life was fuller than his work. He deeply loved his wife and their three small sons.

On the morning of the librarian's thirtieth birthday, he came early to the library. He had been working on some problems connected to the nature of time. Was it a constant? Could it speed up or slow down according to the conditions in which it was kept? The librarian arrived early that morning, so that he might join his family later for a birthday celebration his wife had been planning for months.

But when the librarian opened the huge iron doors to the library, he discovered, sprawled on the marble floor just inside the entrance, the dead body of an old temple priest, a difficult and cynical man with whom the librarian had been fighting for years. The priest had believed that the librarian was meddling in matters that were more properly the province of the gods, or, at the very least, the gods' representatives on earth.

The librarian was frightened. The old man had an enormous gash on the left side of his head. He knew immediately that he would be accused of the murder. In the afternoon of the previous day, the priest had come to the library to meet with the librarian. The meeting had ended in a shouting match. So, finding his nemesis sprawled on the marble floor, the librarian panicked. He gathered up his things and reluctantly went running off into the countryside. He had been raised there, and initially thought that he might hide out for a while until he could sneak back into the kingdom and steal his family away.

As luck, or perhaps the gods, would have it, the librarian wandered for many weeks until he came upon another kingdom. In due course, the librarian took a job as servant to the king. The king was a wise man, one who appreciated the finer things of life. He was immediately impressed with the erudition of the new servant, so he frequently invited the librarian to his table to discuss great works of literature, astronomy, and philosophy. Indeed, there were rumors in the kingdom that many years before the royal family had come from a long line of librarians.

Because of the king's great wisdom, he had made it a habit of dispensing sound advice on matters large and small to anyone in the kingdom, from the lowliest peasant to the highest nobleman. And for the advice, the king always received in return whatever the advisee could afford. Much of the king's time was spent reading, but when he was not reading he usually could be found in the throne room giving the well-needed advice.

Months turned into years, and the years to decades. After working for twenty-five years for the king, the librarian decided he could no longer bear the estrangement from his family and his books, so he told his master that he must leave. The king wisely agreed that the younger man's time had come, and before the librarian left, a party was held in the kingdom, where gifts were brought to the librarian and fine speeches were made about how much he had meant to the monarch and his people. Indeed, the old king gave the librarian an impressive sum, more than 3,000 dinari, for all his years of faithful service to the king and his kingdom.

But just as the librarian was about to depart, the king asked him if he did not want some advice from his former master. "All these years of watching people with heavy hearts come and go, don't you wish a little parting advice from me?" The younger man hesitated a moment, then finally consented to the advice. He had seen how men far less erudite than himself had profited from the king's advice.

"For you, and you alone, I have three pieces of advice," the old man said, "but each will cost you. If you buy the first piece of advice, then you may refuse the other two. But if you purchase the second piece, then you are honor bound to pay for the third."

Again the younger man hesitated. Why had the king put the matter in just this way? But then the librarian looked at the large sack of gold coins he was about to sling over his shoulder. It was a heavy burden, and perhaps if he lightened it a little, he could also take away some fine advice. And so, trusting in the fairness of his former master, he did not ask the price of the advice.

"Your first piece of advice will cost you ten dinari," the king said evenly. The servant set the bag on the ground, and cheerfully retrieved ten dinari and waited for the first piece of advice.

The old man's clear blue eyes looked pensive, as if he had discovered something above and to the right of the librarian's head that, at least for the moment, was the most important thing in the universe. Finally, the old man spoke:

"You must never try a new road until you are sure the old road is a dead end. Neither should you retrace your steps."

The younger man smiled the kind of smile of a man who thinks he may have too quickly parted with ten dinari. But in the next moment he remembered that he still had a fortune left in his sack, not to mention the possibility of two more pieces of advice, which certainly he would find more useful than the first. And so the librarian tentatively retrieved a second ten-dinari coin from the bag.

As he reached for the coin, the king said this:

"Your second piece of advice is also for you alone, but remember you need not purchase it." The younger man hesitated briefly and then dropped the coin in the king's open palm.

"Your second piece of advice is quite simple: remember that a person's life may look very different from the inside than it does from the outside. Thus, you ought always to give others the benefit of the doubt when judging their reasons."

Again the younger man smiled, but it was more like a grin, really—the sort of grin one might imagine on the face of one who has just been taken for twenty dinari. Still, the librarian knew that he had a fortune remaining, and the third piece of advice was bound to be more practical than the other two.

And so, the young man pulled a shinny ten-dinari coin from the sack and handed it to the old king. The old man turned the coin between his fingers, as he smiled for a moment. Then he handed the coin back to the librarian.

"The third piece of advice is the most simple, but it is, at the same time, the most important. But it will cost you 2,970 dinari. Remember your bargain, if you took the first two pieces of advice you are honor bound to pay for the third." And with this, the king ordered one of his servants to remove the sack from the throne room.

The librarian was flushed with rage. "How can you do this? You have taken advantage of me...I have trusted you...for twenty-five years I worked for you...and now it is all for naught."

"But you must keep your side of the bargain," the old man said. "A man of letters, a scholar and librarian, ought to keep his word." The young man stared at the king, and with bitterness mixed with resignation in his voice he asked: "What is it...what is this great pearl of wisdom for which I have paid a fortune?"

Again the old man's eyes looked off into the distance. For the longest of moments he seemed to be trying to make out something on the horizon. Finally, again he spoke:

"The third piece of advice is at once the simplest and the most important: when you are angry, put it away for a day, if the next day your passion still moves you, then you most likely are correct, and then you may act on your anger, but only as much as the situation requires."

The librarian's face again turned crimson. "But a deal is a deal," he thought. "Nevertheless, I will never be taken like this again."

The remainder of the going away party was somber, to say the least. Indeed, it was so somber that no one ate the large cake that had appeared with little pomp from the king's kitchen.

"I see that you and the rest of my subjects are no longer in the proper mood for cake. Here, you must take it with you on your journey, perhaps you might wish to share it with others on another day."

So the librarian picked up the large wooden box, with a royal velvet lining, in which the cake had been placed and he haphazardly placed it in an empty sack with which one of the servants had returned. With the sack slung over his shoulder, the librarian made his way out of the throne room and into the larger world outside the kingdom.

A day into his journey, the librarian met a group of young men who were out to seek adventure. They all had worked for other kings in other kingdoms. All had received parting gifts. Indeed, after comparing stories, it was clear to them that each had been bilked of a great fortune.

The librarian traveled with the men for weeks. They pooled their meager resources, about forty dinari, and with a bit of hunting and fishing, they managed to survive. But through these weeks together, none of the wayfarers thought to bring his gift out to share with the others. One man had received a giant wheel of cheese, which he kept in a sack; a second, an enormous loaf of hard bread; and the third had been given a large box, with a tin clasp, filled with trinkets made of glass. None brought his gift from the sacks they each carried. It was as much out of embarrassment as anything else.

One day the three friends suggested to the librarian that they take a tiny fork in the road, a hilly way that led off into the mountains, rather than the long way around them. But the librarian remembered the advice of the old king: "Don't try a new road until you are sure the old one is a dead end. Neither should you retrace your steps."

"I already have paid for the first piece of advice, what harm would there be in taking it?" the man said to himself. And so, as the librarian stared off in the direction of the open road, he declined to join his friends on the shortcut.

After saying good-bye to the three wayfarers, the librarian set off alone on the old road. But it was not a half an hour later that he heard the clanging of swords and the shouts of men at arms. The young friends, by taking the shortcut, had encountered a band of brigands who quickly killed the three and took their belongings.

For many weeks more the librarian wandered in the countryside. The road led him around the mountains, through a desert, and then on to rich farmland. Presently, he came to an old farm house. The old house, and the rich farmland around it, were owned by an old woman. Inside the house could be found every item of food one could imagine: cheeses, cakes, and meats of every description; breads and an astonishing array of fruits; and the heartiest looking vegetables. But despite the cornucopia to be found in her house, the gaunt old woman sat on her porch, a pensive look on her face, and an impressive crossbow in her lap.

"I wonder if I might buy some food from you?" the librarian asked. "I have been traveling for some time now and I am very hungry. I see in looking through your window that you have a great deal that is nourishing, far more than you could eat in a single lifetime."

"You are right, it is far more than I will ever eat, but you cannot have it for any price," the old woman said, and she raised her bow to scare off the intruder.

The man thought for a moment about how easy it would be to overcome the frail woman. He could deflect her only arrow with his shield and then set upon her, kill her with one swift blow to the head, and then eat all he wanted. This surely would be what the selfish old woman deserves. But a moment later he remembered the king's second piece of advice: "A person's life may look different from the inside than it does from the outside. You must always give people the benefit of the doubt when judging their intentions." With this the man put down his shield and came up on the porch to meet face to face with the old woman.

The woman returned the crossbow to her lap. "You know," she said, "many other wayfarers have died trying to eat the cursed food in my house. They all lie buried out in my fields. They have made good fertilizer for my crops. But you are the first to survive. You are the first to take 'no' for an answer.

"Many years ago an evil sorcerer placed this food in my house, lacing it with poison. He also cast a spell on my fields, so that anything grown there will also contain the poison. So I sit here with this bow to ward off the visitors. It is for their own good. But until now, no one had heeded my warning. I sometimes have fired my arrow at them, trying simply to wound them, but they have warded it off with their shields and then walked into the house for their final meals. The sorcerer has cast a spell over me so that I may only tell the story to those who survive. I could not tell you, nor the others, before hand. In the basket by the door you will find some potatoes, it is all that I have, but you are welcome to half...I have managed to hide the potatoes from the sorcerer."

As the man peeled a potato with his dagger, the old woman told the story of her husband, a man who was once a great scholar and the librarian of a great kingdom. The evil sorcerer had become jealous of the scholar and killed him. In revenge, the woman had tried to lure the sorcerer into eating a poisoned meal. Her plans were thwarted, and the sorcerer exacted his punishment. The old woman said that she no longer needed the crossbow. It seemed rather silly to brandish it. No one ever paid any attention to it. Besides she no longer had the heart to fire it, so she gave the bow, and its magic arrow to her only surviving visitor. "Perhaps you will be able to use it some day," she said with a toothless smile.

The librarian finished his potato, thanked the old woman for saving his life, and then continued on his journey. For months more he wandered. Eventually he came to some mountains which he swore he had seen before, perhaps from another angle. He came to the crest of a hill, and when he peered below, he found his former kingdom, the one where he had left his family behind. At first he was amazed at how little the kingdom had changed. On the edge of the kingdom he could make out his beloved library and also the temple where he had worshipped with his family. He moved stealthily through the streets until he came to the side window of the temple. When he peered in, he discovered his wife, as beautiful as ever, dancing with a young man dressed as a bride groom.

The librarian's face again flushed with rage. He had been away for more than twenty-five years, but hadn't his marriage vows been sacred, were they not eternally binding? Had they not pronounced these solemn vows right in this very temple? How could she marry someone else?

The librarian immediately began to plot his revenge. He would kill them now, while they were both still on the dance floor. He would use the crossbow and its special arrow given him by the old woman. He would kill them both with the magic arrow and then escape again, just as he had the last time.

The librarian loaded the crossbow and prepared to crash open the temple door. But a moment later, he remembered the third piece of advice, the piece of advice for which he had paid a fortune: "Put off your anger for a day..."

"Surely," he said to himself, "I will be no less angry tomorrow than I am today," but in another instant he thought about how the old king's first two pieces of advice had saved his life, and he put down his new weapon. A moment later, from another room, the real bride appeared, young and radiant. The groom was the librarian's son; what he thought was the bride was really the mother of the groom.

When the librarian understood what was going on, he wept silently. A moment later, he opened the temple door and immediately was recognized by all present. It was then that his family told the story of how the old temple priest had died of a heart attack, the wound on his head happened when he struck the marble floor. For years the wife had wondered why the librarian would pick his birthday to run out on his family. But through it all, she knew there was an explanation. And through it all, she had never remarried.

In the intervening years, the oldest son had applied himself to his studies with extra diligence. By the age of twenty-eight he had become the kingdom's finest scholar, as well as its chief librarian. His fiancée was a princess, a most beautiful and desirable young woman, but even on his wedding day, the young man had thought longingly about his missing father.

The older librarian was amazed by the young man's tale, as his family was amazed by his own. But the older librarian still felt embarrassed about having nothing for the wedding couple. Then he remembered the cake in his bag. When he opened the wooden box the cake miraculously had held its shape and freshness. And when the wedding couple sliced the cake with the old librarian's dagger, there tumbled out onto the floor 2,960 dinari.

At first the young couple was amazed at the father's generosity. The new family danced and sang well into the night and early into the next morning. The old librarian also heard the stories of his other two sons. Like their elder brother, they also were preparing themselves to be scholars. Perhaps one day they would become librarians.

But toward day break the old librarian took the bridegroom out into the temple garden to watch the sun rise. With his arm around the young man, and the first rays of the new day's light on the father's face, he said this:

"My son I have been many places and seen some extraordinary things. There is a second part to your wedding present; it is for you and your wife alone. For you I have three pieces of advice. If you accept the first, you need not accept the second; but if you accept the first two pieces, then you are honor bound to accept the third..."

THE SENSE OF TOUCH

In a marriage losing faith in the other
is like losing one's sense of touch.
Rollo May
Man's Search for Himself

Even a man who asks for miracles
would wonder how to live with one
when it came splitting the atom of the known.
Maura Eichner, SSND
"Splitting the Atom of the Known"

My forty-one-year-old brother fell off a roof the other day. He was helping his brother-in-law make some minor repairs. Apparently, he landed face down, putting a big gash in his head, bruising his liver, and causing an assortment of facial lacerations. He also broke his back in two places: one in his neck, the other in the middle of his chest. As I write this, we are not sure of the extent of his paralysis. He cannot move his legs, but he does have limited sensation on both sides of his lower extremities.

While waiting in the shock trauma center for a miracle, I have been thinking of how important and how unheralded is our sense of touch. My father, a man not given to great displays of physical affection—at least not with his sons—took my brother's battered hand in his and held it during our short visits in the intensive care unit and the recovery room. Periodically, my father would kiss the back of his youngest son's hand. Now and then he placed my brother's palm on the side of his weathered face, large tears sliding between hand and cheek. My father did not think about what he was doing. These were involuntary actions. My father intuitively knew that the sense of touch is often all that remains in the most tragic of circumstances.

Since returning to the waiting room, I have been picking through magazines from six months ago. A moment later I see an advertisement for a long distance telephone company featuring Michelangelo's painting of the Sistine Chapel—the creation scene where God stretches out his finger tips to a waiting Adam. There is some distance between the figures, and it is not clear if their fingers ever will connect. Michelangelo seems to have understood the awesome importance of the sense of touch and its power to make the invisible visible.

A few moments later, I begin thinking about my failed marriage. As in many dying relationships, it was the touching that went first, followed by the other feelings. The absence of touching began as a small pin-prick in the middle of the relationship. In time, the hole grew until the marriage was nothing more than a thin border, a frame around the loneliness.

In even the best of marriages, touching has many uses. *Webster's* gives us eleven different uses of the word. An important one the dictionary does not mention is that touching is often a substitute for the things that cannot be seen and cannot be said. When we refuse to say those things, and when the touching has ceased, the space between husband and wife becomes too large and in time it can no longer be called a marriage. Toward the very end, when it is too late, one may even bristle at the touch of the other.

I worry now about my brother's marriage. It is a strong bond, but one where the rules about touching may change. My sister-in-law may live with a man who is able to feel very little from the chest down. But it is the kind of marriage where some of those things left unsaid will now be uttered, over and over, perhaps in the darkest part of the night. It is the kind of relationship where husband and wife always have found a way for spirit to touch spirit. They will find a way to make the invisible visible.

In the meantime, the various members of the family wait and pray, but most of all we touch each other and, in return, we are touched.

THE DAY OF JUDGMENT

*Only our concept of time makes it possible to speak
of the Day of Judgment by that name. In reality, it
is a summary court in perpetual session.*

Franz Kafka
The Trial

*Where were you when I laid the foundations of the
earth? Tell me if you have understanding.*

The Book of Job (38:1)

Many years ago in the city of Copenhagen there lived a great scholar
of ancient Hebrew language and literature. For over half a century
the old man lived alone among his books and fragile manuscripts.
Earlier in life he had been married, but after only a few years of silent
struggle his young wife realized that the most intimate love of which the
scholar was capable was to be found in thoughts and feelings the man
had about the texts he spent his days and nights poring over. Thus, the
couple, if they could be called that, remained childless.

Of all the ancient texts and manuscripts that filled the scholar's
small study, one was, by far, the most valued. It was a tenth century
Hebrew text of the biblical book of Job, prepared and annotated in
the Middle Ages by Rabbi Aaron ben Asher, an illustrious member of
a long family of Hebrew scholars, the Masoretes. It was this particular text that had occupied his attention the day the hack pulled up to
take his wife away. She did not think it prudent nor necessary to leave
the professor a note. She simply told the housekeeper, Mrs. Simpson,
that she would not be returning in the afternoon, and that she should
make sure the professor had his dinner.

In the early nineteenth century, the Asher text had been found in a *geniza*, the storeroom of an old synagogue in Prague. More than a century later, the Danish scholar had come by the manuscript through a series of Byzantine and some would say unsavory twists and turns, involving the Czech government and the Nazi Ministry of Culture. In the past several years, after the professor's wife had gone, the man spent nearly all his time working on this text.

What made this particular Hebrew manuscript so interesting is that it contained an unusual vocalization in the beginning of Chapter 38—God's mysterious speech from the whirlwind—that the scholar never before had seen. He had worked on the passage many times in other texts prepared by the Asher family, but none was like this version. There was a strange diacritical mark, nothing more than a dot really, that appeared in the text just above the most sacred name for God, *Yhwh*. The dot, the professor believed, dramatically changed the import of God's speech. He thought it might indicate that the entire speech, some three full chapters, was to be taken ironically, but he was not yet ready to say for sure.

The scholar's work was complicated these days by the fact that his eyes were failing, and he wondered to himself if he would be given the time needed to finish his work. Thus, the professor began to devise a series of rather clever compensations to aid his sight. He moved his great desk to a space between the two large windows in his study. He employed a second high-intensity light above the desk to illuminate the precious manuscript. He did all he could to give himself the time he needed to complete his inquiry.

After his wife had gone, the only person with whom he had regular contact, contact after a certain fashion at any rate, was Mrs. Sophie Simpson, the housekeeper. Mrs. Simpson had, so to speak, come with the house. She had cooked and cleaned for the previous owners, and helped out with the raising of their children.

Mrs. Simpson was a woman of indeterminate age, younger than the scholar, though she suffered from arthritis and various minor ailments that lately had made her job increasingly more difficult. Indeed, Mrs. Simpson was not at all sure how much longer she would continue. She had a niece in America, a cultural anthropologist, a single mother, who was eager for Mrs. Simpson's expertise. She stayed because she felt sorry for the scholar, and she worried what would happen to him if she were to leave.

But this all changed the day they made the discovery. On that Friday afternoon, Mrs. Simpson had made the scholar's lunch as she always had. And she waited, as she always did, for the man to find a few moments to eat it. Having waited for nearly an hour, finally she rapped lightly on the study door. Through the door, she heard a muffled "come in."

"Mrs. Simpson," he said looking up from the manuscript. He had forgotten to remove the magnifying glass from the head-piece he had fashioned to hold it. This gave the impression to both Mrs. Simpson and to the professor that the eyes of the other were enormous, like those of certain flying insects. For the briefest of moments those enormous eyes met. "There can be no question of dinner," he said. "Look here at this manuscript, I am just on the edge of developing a theory about this particular vocalization."

Mrs. Simpson looked at the man, half-smiling, half-deprecating, that such a small dot should have so completely disturbed the order and meaning of his life. "But sir," she said soothingly, "by now your meal is cold." She looked around the study which she had not been allowed for months to enter. Thick dust had settled on everything but the single text illuminated on the scholar's desk.

In an instant Mrs. Simpson saw her opportunity. With a wave of her arms, and in a voice that surprised her as much as it did the professor, she managed to hurry him out of the study, exacting from him a promise that he would not return from the dimly lighted dining room for at least half an hour.

Mrs. Simpson went to work immediately. While she straightened things, the scholar ate his lunch in the darkened dining room. For an instant he thought of his wife, he fixed on an image of her standing in her wedding dress by a carriage that had transported them to and from the church. But a moment later, he thought about the Asher manuscript, and wondered if there were texts in the Naphtali family of scholars, a rival school, that might hold the key to the mysterious diacritical mark. When he returned to his study, he would begin to check on the matter.

In the meantime, Mrs. Simpson had removed piles of papers from their places on tables, chairs, and the floor, dusted where they had been, and then returned them to their original position. Finally, with feather duster in hand she moved to the great desk between the two windows, through which she could see brown and orange leaves swirling in a tiny whirlwind. She began to run the fine feather duster over the surface of the desk.

As the scholar turned the handle of the study door, Mrs. Simpson blew and dusted the top of the desk. As she did, the vocalization disappeared, for this remarkable dot had been nothing more than a very small, round black bug that had chosen to do its dying on a tenth century Hebrew manuscript.

The scholar never recovered. Mrs. Simpson stayed on for only a few months more, and then she moved to America. A few years later, the manuscript, along with others, was sold at auction to a promising young scholar at Oxford.

The Spider's Star

Habit, if not resisted, soon becomes necessity.
St. Augustine
On Free Will

*The chains of habit are generally too small to
be felt until they are too strong to be broken.*
Samuel Johnson
Letters

In his *Principles of Psychology* William James calls habit "the enormous fly-wheel of society, its most precious conservative agent." James knew that habit builds things: it creates virtue; it makes us good at our jobs; it turns us into dependable parents, spouses, and friends. Habit secures for us a place in the world.

But habit and the all-too-familiar also have the uncanny capacity to waste, and to destroy. Habit, as Miguel de Unamuno has pointed out, is often the first step in ceasing to be. What we have grown accustomed to, after a while, becomes the way things really are. Experience marries memory, and habit becomes its offspring. When habit matures, it rarely leaves home.

The eviction of habit usually comes when someone or something comes between us and the habitual. Often the event is a traumatic one. Divorce, a death in the family, or a tragic accident involving a loved one, all have a way of reminding us that the habitual is a thin veneer we lay over the truly ephemeral nature of things. In this way, habit becomes a great deadener of pain, of hope, or sometimes of a yearning for tenderness we no longer seem to attract or deserve.

But sometimes habit is shown the door in a more subtle way, in a way that involves grace. It often happens in the summertime when the world is full of magic and the smallest of children see it without habit. Only to a magician or a small child is the world eternally new. Only they know the secrets of change, only they know that things are lying in wait, eager to become something else.

Returning to the sea with a small child destroys the habitual. By the ocean, a slight change in routine is sufficient to destroy our daily sense of the way things are; the moment we pass out of our habits we begin to understand again the impermanency of things. At the beach this begins with the shedding of one's clothes.

In the morning, the three-year-old boy and I return from the sea. We stretch out side by side dripping in the sun. I feel my heart beating beneath my bare chest, and I remember for the first time in six months that I have a heart. Back in the city, my heart is not something that occupies my time. In the city, life consists of omnipresent noise, with rare appeals to tiny parcels of silence. Here on the beach, it is quiet enough to hear my heart slow, to listen to its return to a more natural rhythm.

In the afternoon, we walk along the beach. The boy keeps no day-book. Even back in the city, few appointments are made for him. His time is spent living so completely in a series of eternal moments that I spend a good bit of my time pulling him along to meet my schedule.

As we walk, the sea encroaches and recedes, while the boy, accompanied by hungry sandpipers, plays tag with the frothy surf. A moment later he returns to my waiting hand and we discover two black spots moving ahead of us on the beach—they are the shadows of ourselves. Without the habitual, the boy is not sure what to make of the shadows. He reminds me that Peter Pan had a difficult time catching his.

For the rest of the afternoon we talk about dolphins, the sun rising and setting, and the origins of the strange shells of horseshoe crabs tumbling up from the surf. And through all of this I think I am teaching the boy something. I think I am using habit and experience in providing him with a proper view of the way things are. And then in an instant he teaches me to see.

On the way back to the house, on a narrow wooden path the boy finds an industrious spider. The spider has managed to spin an impressive web. When the boy leans down to have a closer look, the web vibrates with a gentle breeze from the west. "Look Daddy," the boy says, "the spider has a wind blowing through his star."

Only goodness meeting evil, and not infected by it, can conquer evil.
Leo Tolstoy
What I Believe

Chapter 5

Goodness Meeting Evil

A Board Game

*Justice consists in seeing that no harm is
done to men. Whenever a man cries
inwardly, "Why am I being hurt?" harm
is being done to him. He is often mistaken
when he tries to define the harm, and why
and by whom it is being inflicted upon him.
But the cry itself is infallible.*

Simone Weil
quoted in W.H. Auden's
A Certain World

*The original position is a hypothetical
situation in which fully rational agents,
unaware of their personal characteristics
or places in society, chose the principles
of distribution that they wish to govern
everyone in society.*

John Rawls
A Theory of Justice

Imagine a board game. The game has many pieces—white, black, yellow, and tan—all representing various players. The board is laid out much like the square playing surface for Monopoly, only much larger and more detailed. There are various economic, educational, and social opportunities, as well as squares representing various human pitfalls, temptations and moral shortcomings all too common to *homo sapiens*. One's fortunes rest both on chance and the intelligence and cunning of each of the players. But before the game begins, each participant must make an arduous trip down a long, dark tunnel into a great light. In the room where the great light is kept, is a pair of dice that must be rolled several times by anyone wishing to enter the game.

The first roll determines if you will be a black piece or a white one, or perhaps yellow or brown. A roll of two through eight signify the white pieces; nine and ten the black; eleven the brown; and twelve the yellow. Thus one has a nearly 60% chance of being one of the white players; a roughly 20% chance of being black; and a little less than 10% each for brown and yellow.

After this first roll, both the white and black pieces are divided into several groups. Each of the black players again rolls one of the dice. If he rolls a one, he must leave the game by his eighteenth turn. If he rolls a two, he is allowed to begin with most of the white players. If he rolls a three, four, or five he must begin five turns after the white players. If he rolls a six, he must go directly to jail. He may avoid jail, however, by agreeing to skip ten turns.

The white players roll in a similar way. If they roll a one, they begin five spaces ahead of the other white players. If they roll a two, three, or four, they begin the game with most of the white pieces; with a roll of five or six, they are placed five places behind the majority of the white players. The white pieces usually get to be the banker.

Similar arcane rules exist for the yellow and brown pieces, as well. There are also a number of mixed color pieces, often they decide their own color but sometimes the rules for their participation become quite complicated—so complicated that we do not have the space nor the cleverness to relate them here.

The third roll in the Room of Light is for one's genetic material. The luck of the roll gives one-sixth of all the players superior intelligence; fourth-sixth average intelligence; and one-sixth below average intelligence. But there are often arguments throughout the game about how the players are to measure or recognize it. Some argue the yellow players get too much of it. In private asides some of the white pieces say that the black pieces rarely are smart enough to play the game well; others that the white pieces too often get to make up the questions.

At the risk of making our game sound too complicated, many of the white pieces are not required to count each of the spaces on the board. Thus, for example, there are eight spaces in the game marked "heart disease: you lose." The white pieces may skip over two of these spaces, while the black pieces are subject to all of them. Similar stipulations exist for other hazards that might prematurely force one from the game.

And thus the game begins. In the course of the game, each player is expected to use his game-given intelligence and cunning; and each is required to advance according to the rules of the game. Often groups of like-colored players begin to act in their collective self-interest. Sometimes this is good for the game as a whole, and sometimes it is not, but mostly it produces other arguments where the different color pieces often shout and call each other names.

Now imagine that after this game has been played for some time, many of the players represented by the black pieces begin to grumble that the game is not fair. And so, after a long while, adjustments are made to the game so that the odds are increased that some of the black players will win more often.

But after a while, other problems arise. Some of these later adjustments to the rules infuriate many of the white players. Eventually enough of the black pieces begin the game on the same square as most of the whites that these angry white players begin to believe that many of the changes in the rules—many of the adjustments made to help the black pieces win more often—no longer are necessary.

They say that some of the newer accommodations given to the more recent black pieces have nothing to do with those black pieces who actually were around when the rules were not so fair. These disgruntled white pieces say that now sometimes the black pieces take double and triple turns when they are not looking. But some of the other white pieces feel guilty because they think the rules never really have been fair, and they don't know what to do about it. Many of them wring their hands while they wait for their next turn. After a while, it is hard to find any trust between the white pieces and the black. This is the major reason why they never land or stay on the "leisure" and "fun" squares at the same time. And neither group ever hangs out with the brown or the yellow either.

After a while, the ways in which the participants see the game itself are so different that there are various complaints from all quarters about the basic fairness of the game. But no one playing the game seems to know how to go about doing anything constructive about those complaints.

Now after you have imagined all this, then imagine anyone wanting to play this game if they were given a full description of the rules before hand. Suppose you were invited to play but you did not know which color piece you would be before giving your permission to participate. Would you play this game? Would you sign up not knowing which color piece you would be? Or would you wait to play until the rules got straightened out a little better?

Dr. Death: The Messenger and the Message

A good death does honor to an entire life.

Petrarch

Canzoniere

You know who is scared? The intelligentsia at the top,
because their empire is crumbling. Medicine and the editorial
writers and the judiciary are all in cahoots. I'm not off my
rocker. I'm different. But so was Freud. They're saying the
same about me, word for word.

Jack Kevorkian

US News and World Report

August 27, 1990

Kevorkian: The Messenger

On a warm, muggy evening in August, 1993, Thomas Hyde, a thirty-year-old construction worker, along with his wife and two-year-old daughter, sat inside a battered and rusted 1968 VW bus parked behind an apartment complex in Detroit's suburban Royal Oak. Mr. Hyde suffered from amyotrophic lateral sclerosis, Lou Gehrig's disease. He had come to Royal Oak for one purpose: to end his life with the help of the VW's owner, Dr. Jack Kevorkian.

After fitting an oxygen mask over Mr. Hyde's head, Dr. Kevorkian connected the tubing leading from the mask to a small cylinder of carbon monoxide. Half-way down the tubing, Dr. Kevorkian had placed a paper clip that crimped the line, preventing the deadly flow of CO. To the paper clip, the then sixty-five-year-old retired pathologist Kevorkian had attached a string which he handed to Mr. Hyde. A moment later, after saying good-bye to his wife and daughter, Mr. Hyde pulled loose the paper clip, breathed in the carbon monoxide, and died.

Thomas Hyde was the twentieth person to be assisted by Dr. Kevorkian into that Great Night. Since the summer of 1993, the pathologist has assisted in another 110 people ending their lives. The most recent of these deaths, however, was different in kind. On September 17, 1998, after ushering family out of the house so that they would not be implicated, Dr. Kevorkian administered lethal drugs through an IV to Thomas Youk, a fifty-two-year-old accountant who also was suffering from Lou Gehrig's disease. This was the first known case in which Dr. Kevorkian was the direct causal agent in the death of one of his "patients." The death scene was videotaped by the pathologist and shown on *60 Minutes* during the important last week of November "sweeps" when viewer levels are measured to set advertising rates. The Nielsen Media Research company reported that an estimated 15.6 million households tuned in to the death, the highest numbers for the show this season.

It is undeniable that all Dr. Kevorkian's 130 "patients" have gone gently, but it is less clear that they, and their pathologist assistant, have done the morally right thing in these sorrowful cases. It is still less clear that Dr. Kevorkian has had the motives he professes in helping others into what Henry James aptly called "The Great Perhaps." Although he claims a staunch altruism with respect to the suffering of the terminally ill, as well as a reverence for the autonomy of the individual, one might well conclude that Kevorkian has had, for many years, a bizarre and unhealthy interest with death and the newly dead. Contrary to his stated altruistic goals in assisting and now administering gentle death, Dr. Kevorkian may well be playing out a strange self-interested fascination with the dead, an interest that stretches back to his early medical training in Michigan.

Dr. Kevorkian was first called "Dr. Death" while a resident at the Detroit Receiving Hospital. It was there in 1956 that he began photographing the retinas of patients at the moment of death. He set up his camera equipment and waited. He called the process his "death rounds." A few years earlier, in 1953, Dr. Kevorkian had been dismissed from the University of Michigan pathology residency because of his proposal that death-row inmates be rendered unconscious rather than executed, so that their bodies could be used for extended medical experiments. When the experiments were completed, Dr. Kevorkian suggested, the inmates could be declared dead.

In 1959, at a meeting of the American Association for the Advancement of Science, Dr. Kevorkian read a paper entitled: "Capital Punishment or Capital Gain?" in which he again argued that death-row inmates be anesthetized so that their living bodies could be used for scientific experiments that could last "for hours or even months." A few years later in April of 1966, Dr. Kevorkian testified before a joint judiciary committee in Columbus, Ohio. The pathologist urged the state of Ohio to revamp its capital punishment laws so that "valuable medical experiments" might be performed on the condemned.

In the 1960s, Dr. Kevorkian developed an interest in oil painting, completing nearly two dozen large canvases later lost in a move from California back to his native Michigan. Photographs of the paintings reveal the fruits of his artistic labors: large brush strokes with bold colors, featuring the unmistakable likenesses of dismembered corpses and other apparent victims of torture and mutilation. In a 1991 interview with Kevorkian, writer Michael Betzold describes the paintings as "striking, gruesome, surrealistic visions full of skulls and body parts, cannibalism, and harsh religious parody." In a 1993 profile of the pathologist for the *New York Times*, Kevorkian told Jack Lessenberry, "I never called them art, but philosophy in paint."

Some might argue that these assembled facts add up to little more than an *ad hominem* argument against Dr. Kevorkian—a kind of killing the messenger. But what if the messenger has an overactive interest in gentle killing? Indeed, a careful examination of the facts surrounding many of Kevorkian's "patients" lead one to ominous conclusions. The first of Kevorkian's 130, Janet Adkins, a fifty-four-year-old Oregon woman with Alzheimer's disease, used an early version of the drug "Thanitron" to kill herself on June 4, 1990. Ms. Adkins had played several sets of tennis the afternoon before her death in the back of Kevorkian's van. The body of Kevorkian's second "patient," Marjorie Wantz, a fifty-eight-year-old woman who complained of unremitting pelvic pain, was found by the Oakland County, Michigan medical examiner to have no signs of disease.

Hugh Gale, a seventy-year-old sufferer from congestive heart failure and emphysema—and the thirteenth of Kevorkian's "cases"—died by carbon monoxide poisoning on February 15, 1993. In addition to Dr. Kevorkian's presence, Mr. Gale's death also was attended by his wife, Cheryl Gale, and by Margo Janus and Neal Nicol, two of the Michigan pathologist's assistants. A short time after Gale's death, members of the anti-abortion group Operation Rescue purported to find a document in Mr. Nicol's trash indicating that during the procedure Gale had asked twice for the oxygen mask to be removed. Later, in a search of Dr. Kevorkian's Royal Oak apartment, a similar document was found by the police with a line of type that had been whited-out and typed over, eliminating any mention of Mr. Gale's misgivings. In a subsequent trial Kevorkian dismissed the obscured line as a typographical error, though both Mrs. Gale and Mr. Nicol, after being offered immunity, indicated that Mr. Gale's protests twice were ignored by Dr. Kevorkian.

In August of 1997, Kevorkian assisted in the death of seventy-three-year-old Janet Good, a longtime activist in local and state-wide Michigan politics. For several years prior to her death, Ms. Good had assisted Dr. Kevorkian in his crusade. Indeed, Ms. Good was charged along with the pathologist with assisted suicide in the 1996 death of Loretta Peabody, a fifty-four-year-old sufferer from multiple sclerosis. At an initial hearing in May of 1997, charges were dropped against Ms. Good when she revealed that she was suffering from terminal pancreatic cancer and most likely would not last until the trial. Three months later, Ms. Good was dead in a suicide assisted by Dr. Kevorkian. In an autopsy conducted by Dr. Kanu Virani at the Oakland (Michigan) Medical Examiner's Office, he found no visible signs of disease in any of Ms. Goods organs, including her pancreas.

On March 2, 1998, Roosevelt Dawson, a twenty-one-year-old Smithfield College student who was paralyzed from the neck down, died with the assistance of Dr. Kevorkian. Mr. Dawson, who died with his supportive mother at his side, was not terminally ill. In a subsequent interview the mother spoke of Kevorkian's methods as a logical alternative to living with disabilities.

Over and against these assembled facts—a grisly mosaic that suggests that there is more pathology in Dr. Kevorkian than simply his former medical specialty—is another unassailable fact: three times

the state of Michigan has charged Jack Kevorkian with assisted suicide, and three times the state has failed to win a conviction. More
than anything, this fact speaks to an ambivalence shared by the culture as a whole about moral issues at the end of life. These issues are
important and complex. They cut to the very heart of the nature and
meaning of life and its relationship to suffering.

Thomas A Kempis, in his fifteenth century *Imitatio Christi*, suggests that if one could be still in suffering and let it abide for a while,
then no doubt he would see the help of God come to him. It is clear
that some see Dr. Kevorkian as an angel of mercy, an agnostic sent by
God to relieve intractable suffering. But I wonder about the pathologist's motives. And I wonder if a rational and clear-headed discussion
of these sensitive issues has not been pushed back significantly by
this frail and volatile man, a man with an overactive interest in the
dying and the dead.

Kevorkian: The Message

On May 2, 1994, a Michigan jury found Dr. Jack Kevorkian not
guilty of assisted suicide in the death of Thomas W. Hyde, a thirty-
year-old construction worker and sufferer from Lou Gehrig's disease.
In three subsequent trials, the state of Michigan also failed to gain a
conviction of the retired pathologist. As one juror commented after
the initial proceedings, "He convinced us he was not a murderer, that
he was really trying to help people out." A second juror at the first
trial said that "Dr. Kevorkian had acted principally to relieve Mr.
Hyde's pain, not to kill him, and that is an action within the law." In
Kevorkian's later trials, several jurors also expressed skepticism and
resentment that the state wished to legislate decisions at the end of
life. "I don't feel it is our obligation to choose for someone else how
much pain and suffering they can go through," one said. "That is
between them and their God."

In March, 1999, in Oakland County, Michigan, Dr. Kevorkian, acting as his own attorney, went on trial for the fifth time. This new
indictment, which was handed down in early December of 1998,
came as the result of a videotape that appeared on CBS's *60 Minutes*
on November 22. In an interview that accompanied the tape, Dr.

Kevorkian admitted ending the life of Thomas Youk, a fifty-two-year-old Michigan accountant suffering from Lou Gehrig's disease. In the interview with CBS's Mike Wallace, Kevorkian called Youck's death "my first euthanasia," distinguishing it from Kevorkian's other cases where the pathologist simply provided the means for people to end their own lives.

In this new indictment, prosecutors again charged Kevorkian with assisted suicide, but they also added the charge of murder. But later Oakland County prosecutor David Gorcyca decided to drop the assisted suicide count, leaving only the murder charge. The prosecutor's decision followed a ruling by Oakland County Circuit Court Judge Jessica Cooper that the assisted suicide charge would allow Kevorkian to present evidence from the families of other patients about their pain and suffering. Such testimony would be inadmissible with only the murder charge remaining.

What are we to make of this strange crusader for the rights of the dying? How are we to come to grips with important issues that are brought to the floor for public debate by a man who even his supporters admit is a strange amalgam of B.T. Barnum and the Grim Reaper? What, if anything, has Dr. Death to teach us about the contemporary culture in which we live, and in which we die?

Perhaps the most important lesson we have to learn from Dr. Kevorkian's clashes with the legal system is just how ambivalent we are about assisted suicide and euthanasia. The fact that Kevorkian was not convicted in three separate trials speaks volumes about our culture's deep double-mindedness. In a March 1996 *Washington Post* poll on these issues, 51% of Americans interviewed favored physician assisted suicide (54% of men and 47% of women). But a more interesting set of statistics garnered from the same poll has received far less attention from the national news media. Although 55% of white Americans favored physician assisted suicide, only 20% of African American respondents favored Kevorkian's methods and morals. While 57% between the ages of forty and forty-nine approved of physician assisted suicide, only 35% of respondents over seventy did. An even more telling figure is the mere 37% of people under the poverty line who favored physician assisted suicide.

There are, perhaps, many ways to understand these figures, but one important interpretation that ought not to be discounted is that those members of our society who have traditionally been on the margins (blacks and the elderly, for example) are quite suspicious about how the American health care industry intends to resolve the problem of shrinking resources and spiraling costs. These varying attitudes toward physician assisted suicide mirror the disparate attitudes whites and blacks have in general about their trust of physicians and other health care professionals.

A third lesson we might learn from Dr. Kevorkian is the fact that there is a gap between the legal and medical options actually open to people at the end of life and what physicians, health care-workers, and family members think the alternatives are. In one recent study of physician and health care professionals' attitudes toward end-of-life decision making, more than 40% were unaware that the courts have repeatedly upheld the right of individuals to discontinue feeding tubes and hydration.

In another study, seventy-one patients were moved from critical care units to nursing homes. In twenty-five of these cases, the patients had signed living wills but these advance directives were not sent along with the rest of the patients' charts. As a result, these people were often given treatment they earlier had expressly declined, treatments for which their families later often were held financially responsible,

A fourth realization that Kevorkian may well have brought is that the medical profession has for years been geared to preserving life at all costs. It has not developed ways of dealing with death in cases where it is inevitable and desirable. Rather than aggressively treating all terminal illnesses, we need to concentrate instead on making some people with these illnesses pain free, so that they might spend their remaining time making sense out of the lives lost. In a recent study of 4,000 patients who died after hospital intervention, 40% reported that they were in pain "most of the time" during their treatment. The tragic irony of these statistics is that although significant medical advances are now being made in the treatment of pain, those advances do not always translate into more effective management of pain in care for the dying. In the report of a 1994 New York State Task Force on Life and the Law, the task force members wrote, "Taken together modern pain relief techniques can alleviate pain in all but extremely rare cases," and yet the opposite impression—that intractable pain is inevitable in terminal illness—is most often the point of view held by the general public.

If Dr. Kevorkian has taught us a great deal about how we live and die, he also has misled us on a number of matters. The retired pathologist frequently points to Holland as a more enlightened culture when it comes to end-of-life issues. In 1993 the Netherlands passed legislation establishing specific rules by which physicians could assist terminal patients in their deaths. But the Dutch experience may be far more mixed than Dr. Kevorkian would have us believe. In a recent report by the Royal Dutch Medical Society, the Dutch government acknowledged that the original guidelines are no longer being adhered to. Annually nearly 4,000 people now die in Holland by physician assisted suicide. Of those cases, an estimated 1,000 are non-voluntary euthanasia, acts expressly forbidden by the Dutch policy but never prosecuted.

A 1994 Dutch medical commission also recommended the inclusion of psychiatric patients in the guidelines for those covered by the physician assisted suicide law. The subsequent increase in the number of suicides in Holland recently has led two noted Dutch attorneys to observe: "The creep toward involuntary euthanasia and mercy killing in the Netherlands has gone unchecked, despite legal conditions designed to guarantee voluntariness."

The Dutch experience leads us to another way in which Kevorkian has misled us. The retired pathologist presents his typical "patient" as a rational, thoughtful person who has made an independent decision to end his life, a kind of modern day Socrates willing to drink the hemlock. In most of his recent interviews, Dr. Kevorkian has stressed pain relief as the most important aspect in assisting these people. He argues frequently that the people he helps can no longer stand the pain, and thus make a choice of quality over quantity of life. But a study in the state of Washington, which along with Oregon has the strongest pro-physician-assisted-suicide constituencies in the country, only 31% of terminally ill patients listed pain relief as the most important motivating factor in their desires for death. Seventy-five percent of the same patients in the Washington study listed "not wishing to be a burden" as their principal reason for desiring physician assisted suicide.

A profile of a more typical candidate desirous of physician assisted suicide is an elderly depressive female who thinks of herself as a burden to others. Indeed, of Dr. Kevorkian's first forty-three patients, twenty-eight were women, many of whom were not suffering from terminal illnesses at all. None of these "patients" received a competent psychiatric evaluation before giving themselves over to Dr. Death.

In the final analysis, perhaps the most disturbing aspect of the Kevorkian affair is not the self-promotional atmosphere he brings to these tragic cases, nor is it his obvious lack of empathy for Mr. Youck and others in their dying moments. The most distressing part of these stories is how much they remind us of an age now lost. Before the advent of modern medicine, we died early and often. Death was something integrated into the lives of those left behind. We thought we were going somewhere then, and our destination had a kind of metaphysical and moral sense to it. In this age gone by if we had anxieties about death, they were fears of condemnation. Now with our more sophisticated post-modern sensibilities, guilt has all but disappeared. And, in the process, so often has meaning.

In *Death Comes to the Archbishop*, novelist Willa Cather suggests, "Men travel faster now, but I do not know if they go to better things." If Dr. Kevorkian has his way, we all may be traveling faster to death, but it is not clear that our age is one that believes we go on to better things.

(On March 26, 1999, Dr. Jack Kevorkian was convicted of second degree murder and delivery of a controlled substance.)

THE NEW HOPE MIRACLE

We are all potentially such sick men.
The sanest and best of us are of one
clay with lunatics and prison inmates.
And whenever we feel this, such a
sense of the vanity of our voluntary
career comes over us, that all our
morality appears as a plaster hiding
a sore that can never cure.

William James

Letters

Not all great miracles are great mysteries.

Herman Melville

Moby Dick

The *New Hope* left port just before the New Year, 1619, with a full crew of Hollanders and a full cargo of black gun powder. The Dutch ship, on its way to the East Indies, was under the command of Captain William Bontekoe, as simple and severe a man as his crisp and straightforward narrative from which this story comes. Bontekoe had that vague uneasiness common to children whose parents have not always kept their troubles to themselves. As quickly as he could, at the age of fourteen he ran away from home. He had spent his entire adult life at sea, never marrying, nor passing his austere love for the sea to a next generation.

For months of this final voyage the *New Hope* was met by gales blowing from the south, followed by mysterious lulls sometimes lasting as long as a week. By late November, they had been attacked by

Spanish pirates three times. Captain Bontekoe had lost four of his best men in the confrontations.

Earlier in the summer, they were hit by a tropical storm that the taciturn captain mentions in his log as having waves of thirty feet or more. Six more unfortunate souls fell overboard in two of the largest storms. One man died in his own bunk. Throughout the night many men had clung to the mast and whispered useless prayers in Dutch.

But through all this, most had lived to tell the tale, and on the evening of November 29, 1699, Captain Bontekoe ordered a double portion of rum to be served with the crew's evening meal. The ship's purveyor was sent to the hold to secure two large wooden buckets of rum to be drained from a barrel kept under lock and key. The barrel was kept in a storage bin away from the gun powder.

But the weather was rough, the ship listed to the port side, and the long-wick candle the purveyor was carrying fell into the open barrel of spirits. There was a momentary pause, while a cold aquamarine wave ran up the purveyor's spine. For another instant, he wondered if the flame might miraculously have been extinguished by the wetness of the rum—and then there was the first explosion, followed by an irregular series of larger blasts as the four separate sections of the hull containing the four thousand barrels of gun powder exploded. The ship burned and sank in fifty feet of water in a matter of twelve minutes.

The purveyor, of course, did not live long enough to see the miracle that did transpire. Three sailors, a twelve-year-old cabin boy, and Captain Bontekoe all were spared. A small life boat had been cut loose from the mother ship by the force of the initial blast. All five were thrown to safety, and clamored aboard the dinghy. They had no water, nor food, and the pitiless tropical sun beat down on them for a week.

Captain Bontekoe sat to the rear of the life boat. By the end of the first week, all the men had high fevers. A sailor named Red Joost grabbed the cabin boy Tom by his red hair, and, armed with a curved knife—and crazed by the sea and the sun— the sailor was poised to cut the throat of the freckle-faced cabin boy.

The captain's sparse chronicle ends here, but we do know from later accounts that all four men, as well as the cabin boy, survived. Making a sail from their shirts the five drifted for another six searing days after the sailor drew his blade. Eventually, on the morning of the seventh day, they sighted land. There are three separate and contradictory oral accounts of how the boy's life was spared. To this day, all three tales continue to circulate throughout the Netherlands in separate mythopoetic traditions.

According to the first version, the account told from many pulpits, Captain Bontekoe gave an impassioned speech full of biblical imagery. He reminded Joost, and the other sailors as well, of the story of Abraham and his son Isaac in the twenty-second chapter of Genesis, and of the New Testament account of the slaughter of the innocents, a print of which, all agree, had hung in the Captain's cabin. It is said that the captain finished his appeal with a reminder of what Jesus must have endured in the Garden of Gethsemene. It was these allusions, it is said, that brought the men to their senses and Red Joost to his knees in the center of the small boat.

In the second account, a story told mostly by older sailors and those pretending to be, the captain made a pragmatic bargain with Joost and the others. If they did not manage to reach solid ground in another week, they would kill and eat the boy. The captain assured the other men that he would kill the boy himself. For six days the boy seemed fated to die, but on the morning of the seventh day they sighted land, and the boy's life, as well as those of the others, were saved.

But the third version was, by far, the most complicated of the three. In this account it said that when Joost drew his knife the captain jumped to his feet and shouted that whoever dared touch a hair on the boy's head would be denied, upon their return, his daily pay and food ration. Moreover, if the boy were killed the captain would see to it that the murderer or murderers would be hanged in the center square of Amsterdam, among the jeering and derision of the city's finest citizens.

This was, of course, an abstract threat. They had no way of knowing that in another six days of drifting and blistering they miraculously would be thrown up on dry land by the great sea—that the ocean would deliver them out of its womb and they would crawl reborn onto an island of white sand and mangos. And yet, in this account, the men heed the captain's warning.

Those who tell this version of the tale perhaps know more than the others about why people behave the way they do. While the first variation appeals to the intrinsic goodness of the sailors, the second assumes an underlying ruthless self-interest. But neither of these views has ever given us a full accounting of what might be expected from *homo sapiens*. Original sin or Hobbes' frightening state of nature makes no more sense than Rousseau's myth of noble savages.

This third version is surely the most subtle telling of the tale. It takes into account two truths about humanity. It is not important to reveal them here. Those who know these two truths understand why the third account is the more subtle of the three. Indeed, sometimes these men debate among themselves just what the two truths are. These same men often point out to each other that those who do not know the two truths are rarely thought to understand the real nature of irony.

At any rate, to this day, all three accounts are told and retold in various quarters of the Netherlands.

THE CONGRESSIONAL CHARIOT

The soul is so often at odds with itself.
Edith Stein
Letters

Good is that which makes for unity.
Evil is that which separates us.
Aldous Huxley
Ends and Means

In one of the best of his dialogues, *The Phaedrus*, Plato introduces us to a compelling metaphor for the nature of the human soul. Through his teacher, Socrates, Plato tells us that the soul is like a chariot, its charioteer, and the two horses that make it move. One horse, what Plato calls the appetitive part of the soul, is a dark, passionate steed, without direction. It runs chaotically, acting on its emotions, The other horse, the spirited element of the soul, is docile, obedient, always doing what it is told. The spirited part of the soul runs straight, because others do, even when there is a curve in the road.

Plato warns us that if the chariot is guided by either of its horses, only disaster will follow. If the appetitive horse takes the lead, the chariot careens off the road, ending in a violent crash. If the spirited element is left to do the guiding, the chariot flies off the road at the next bend. In order for the chariot to function as it should, it must be guided by the charioteer, that rational part of the soul.

In Plato's view, it is the rational element of the soul that is capable of apprehending the moral good, so it is also the rational part of the soul that ought to be doing the driving. Indeed, Plato suggests that when the rational function of the soul chooses to give up the reins to one or the other elements, it nevertheless ought to be held responsible for any subsequent damage caused by the chariot. It is the charioteer's job to make a unity of the soul. When this unity is not achieved, evil so often follows.

In this brilliant metaphor, Plato brings us to an understanding of why we are often so double-minded in life's decisions. Our emotions and passions pull us one way; reason or the judgment of others, another. Freud thought this Platonic metaphor so illuminating, he included it in his lecture, "The Question of Lay Analysis," where he searched for the most apt image of the nature of the self. This same image of the chariot and the charioteer also can be found in the ancient Hindu *Katha Upanisad*, as well as in the early Buddhist classic, *The Questions of King Milinda*.

I began to think about Plato's image from *The Phaedrus* the other day while watching the impeachment debate in the House of Representatives. It is, of course, quite risky to make judgments about the souls of others, but I could not help but think of the appropriateness of Plato's metaphor in describing the proceedings in Washington. The entire city, and the nation and the world, are transfixed with these issues because a very powerful man let the wrong horse do the driving. And now, in the aftermath, passion, not reason, seems to rule the day. When it does not, the spirited horse—the part of the self that follows along with the crowd—seems to be guiding the Congressional chariot.

On one side of the aisle, the passionate resentment of President Clinton is nearly palpable. On the other side, the lock-step tendency to follow the party mantra that "it was wrong, but does not rise to the level of an impeachable offense," is just as notable. One side seems ruled by its passions, the other by a tendency to follow along with the defense of a collection of sins, both mortal and venial, simply because the party requires it. And in these two tendencies, where is reason to be found?

Ruled by emotions and unbridled animus, conservative Republicans seem bent on killing what they see as a dangerous bull in a delicate china shop, but they propose to do it with a series of hand grenades. The Democrats vainly try to separate private judgment and character from public life, from civic life, and thus from communal life. This is surely as futile as it is unwise. The late-comers, moderate Republicans, hold their wet index fingers in the air, judging the strength and direction of the moral and political winds, until finally they do what all the other Republicans already unwisely have done. And all seem to do it in such a self-satisfied, glib way.

The only two facts that are certain about the outcome of all this is that we can expect all the parties involved principally to act in their own narrow self-interest, while claiming to vote their consciences. Plato's student, Aristotle, reminds us that all ethics is social. All but the most isolated of moral choices involve the interests of others. When emotions strike out on their own, unaided by reason and judgment, only disaster will follow. When immoral acts are defended because they are private, it makes a mockery of the social conditions under which an oath is taken, whether it be to one's spouse or to the nation on inauguration day. When scores are settled in the name of justice, the chariot moves closer to the brink.

And who in all this is charged with keeping the chariot on the road? Where are those reasonable souls who wish to punish the man while not crippling the office? If a charioteer is to be found in this sordid tale, it is in the will of the people. If reason is speaking in this story, it is in the polls. About two thirds of all Americans think the President has done something seriously wrong, something for which he should be punished. But these same people think that impeachment is a punishment that is woefully unfit for the crime. It is about time that someone listens to reason. The chariot is running off the road.

GENTLE VENGEANCE

Gentle vengeance may be easier for the exactor, but is it better?
Aeschylus
Seven Against Thebes

Revenge holds the cup to the lips of another
but drinks the dregs itself.
Josh Billings
His Works Complete

F lint Gregory Hunt is dead. In 1987, on a bitterly cold night, he
killed Vincent Adolfo, a twenty-five-year-old police officer, with a
new wife and everything to live for. Hunt shot Adolfo in the chest,
and then coldly, dispassionately, he shot him a second time in the
back, at close range.

Twelve years later, on the day after Hunt became the first person in
Maryland to die by lethal injection, I began thinking of a seventeenth
century Dutchman, Jan Barneveldt, whose head was chopped off by a
state executioner on a cool Spring day in 1617.

On the day he died, Barneveldt was led to the platform, where the
hooded executioner hastily rearranged the chopping block, so that
Barneveldt might die with the sun in his face. Some witnesses reported that the executioner leaned over to the condemned man whose
head was in the block and softly said, "At least you shall die with the
sun shining on you." But other witnesses were equally adamant that
the executioner whispered, "I am happy you shall die with the sun in
your eyes." Some saw the executioner's act as a special form of derision—adding the sun's blinding insult to the blade's lethal injury,

while others saw in the act an expression of charity, an odd kind of grace breaking through with the light.

Whatever the truth, there was much debate at the time about whether the executioner had performed his duties properly. The qualities of a good executioner, many argued, depended on the ability to dispatch his responsibilities quickly, efficiently and, above all, dispassionately.

Today we might be inclined to say that Barneveldt's executioner broke his grim fraternity's unwritten code of professional ethics. Whether it was a tender impulse of the heart, or a special act of derision delivered in a man's dying moment, we cannot say. The executioner had delegated to himself a speaking part in the drama of Barneveldt's death. And thus he would forever remain a curious and ambiguous sign of gratuitous insult or perhaps hopeless kindness.

Witnesses to Flint Gregory Hunt's execution remarked that it was like watching a man fall asleep. When Hunt went gently into that great night, like Barneveldt's executioner, the state of Maryland had changed its rules. Earlier Hunt had insisted on dying by the gas chamber, so, as he said, "people could see it for the murder it is." But later, at the eleventh hour, he changed his mind, and only with an appeals court ruling was he permitted to die by lethal injection.

Lethal injection. It has all the moral ambiguity of Barneveldt's executioner. It is like a falling asleep. But is this gentleness offered for the murderer or for the executioners? Does making it easier to die ease one set of primitive passions associated with a natural aversion to blood and death, only to be replaced with a less articulate but warmer passion, a kind of gentle vengeance?

The gas chamber, the firing squad, the electric chair: they look too much like the cold evil committed by Flint Gregory Hunt. Lethal injection is like falling asleep. And in this gentle falling, we try in mid-air to perform a strange moral calculus, where one life magically equals another, one family's searing pain is to be accompanied by another's, not replaced by it. It is a strange addition. But killing is also always a subtraction, no matter who is doing the calculating. Killing does not add life, not even gentle killing.

SEEING STARRS

What other dungeon is so dark as one's own heart?
What jailer so inexorable as one's self?
Nathaniel Hawthorne
Red Badge of Courage

There is no witness so terrible—no accuser so powerful—
as conscience which dwells within us.
Sophocles
Oedipus at Colonus

If the Starr Report were a subject of moral philosophy, what kind of footprint would it leave? I am tempted to say simply "a slimy one," and leave it at that. But this clearly will not do, for the Starr Report has not left a single footprint, but many—and these footprints have been tracked through the middle of our living rooms, classrooms, newsrooms, supermarkets, and houses of worship. These tracks have been made by Mr. Clinton, Mr. Starr, Ms. Lewinsky, and her erstwhile friend, Linda Tripp. More footprints in this story still are to be made by members of Congress. In the end, the shoes in this sordid tale will have been of a variety of sizes, but each will have tracked its own peculiar kind of dirt through what used to be called the American polity.

What sense might we make of this report beyond the fact that its authors are prone to the split infinitive and to the separation of complex verbs? Are there any moral lessons to be learned from 445 pages that read like a cross between lines written by Erica Jong, fresh from anatomy class, and something out of Nathaniel West's *Miss Lonely Hearts*? Is there anything of moral significance to be said about one man who seems prone to falling repeatedly into the same libidinal well, and another man who appears to have derived his rules of legal engagement from Saint Augustine's just war theory? There is sordidness here, but is there illumination?

Let us begin with Mr. Clinton. What can be said of the man from a moral perspective? There are the obvious things. He is the President of the United States who seems intent on stepping on the same moral rake over and over again. He has yielded repeatedly to the same temptation that so many powerful American men often do. President Clinton is a man around whose head the black birds of temptations are quite plentiful, and he unwisely, and fairly regularly, allowed some of them to land.

But the deeper moral questions about Mr. Clinton are at the level of character, not actions, and much of what we might learn about Mr. Clinton's moral character is, at the same time, complex and disturbing. To understand the complexity of it, think for a moment about the President's confession on national television, just moments after giving his grand jury testimony. By nearly everyone's account, the President's few sentiments of contrition that evening were not believable. To understand why, we must think about the nature of Mr. Clinton's character.

Mr. Clinton is incapable, I think, of feeling genuine guilt, the kind of emotion one feels when one is genuinely disappointed in the self. Guilt is indispensable for the living of a moral life. It is quite different from its companion, shame. Shame comes as the result of others finding fault with us. It is a judgment made from the outside. Guilt, the genuine kind, is a judgement made from within. People incapable of guilt will act morally only when someone is watching. When they are convinced they will not be caught, then they see themselves as having *carte blanche* to commit immoral acts. People incapable of genuine guilt are often quite dangerous. When those bereft of guilt are also highly intelligent, then they are particularly dangerous. They are dangerous in two principal ways. First, they know how to act so that they look like they are remorseful, even though they are not. This allows them to appear trustworthy and penitent to others. And secondly, those incapable of guilt rarely change, for there is nothing there at their moral centers.

I think President Clinton's expression of remorse the evening of his deposition seemed insincere because it was. If we could read a subtext that might have existed just below the surface of that speech, I think it would say something like this: "I am very sorry I got caught. And the reason I am sorry is because of what you have found out about me. If I had not gotten caught, I would not be bothered by this."

If we consider what the President said during his first presidential campaign about having smoked marijuana, but not having inhaled, it follows a similar kind of pattern. When the press finally cornered Mr. Clinton about his drug use, he gave an ambiguous answer about trying marijuana a few times, but not having inhaled. Like the Lewinsky confession, this is an admission without a trace of genuine guilt.

The President's suggestion that we ought to "get this behind us" and focus on the business of the country is another piece of the character puzzle. The notion that he and we could put this unsavory business behind us is spoken with a shamed voice, not by a man of conscience. Indeed, one might well ask how a genuinely guilty man is able to shave in the morning. A genuinely guilty man, at least for some time, cannot put immoral choices behind him, for the man who made those choices is looking at him every morning through the bathroom steam. The desire to get so easily something behind him suggests there is something important missing at the core. They are the sentiments of a man who has jumped but wishes you to think he's been pushed.

And what of the other actors in this $45 million drama. Is there anything to be said of Kenneth Starr beyond the realization that he may well be a man who kills house flies with a ten pound maul?

What are we to make of a man who spends years investigating a land deal, a suspicious suicide and other possible acts of malfeasance, finds nothing to report and resigns, then returns to write a 150,000 word document detailing the most intimate details—the wheres and whens—of the President of the United States' bodily fluids?

Monica Lewinsky and Linda Tripp fare no better in a moral analysis. There are no tragic heroes here, but there is lots of hubris to go around. Iago taught us much about deception and its unsavory uses with intimates. But suppose we say that Ms. Tripp is a good Iago; who but saints would want her as a friend? And Ms. Lewinsky? What are we to make of her moral compass? Aristotle, 2500 years ago, gave us a startlingly clear definition of moral responsibility. One is morally blameworthy, he suggests, when one intends to do wrong, knows it is wrong, and could have kept from doing it.

This analysis might apply to having sex with a married man, and to threatening blackmail later. Ms. Lewinsky told us, through her spokeswoman, that she is looking forward to the business of rebuilding her life. When I heard these words I could not help but think of the Three Little Pigs, particularly the one who built his house out of straw. I wonder if he looked forward to the business of rebuilding his life, and whether he thought it prudent to use better materials next time?

I am still waiting for Ms. Lewinsky to apologize for her role in pushing back any discussion of real, substantive moral dilemmas in this country, like affordable health care for everyone, or building schools where American children regularly perform as well as those in other developed nations.

And then there are the rest of us, members of a culture with the moral sensibilities that seem constructed from a few parts Calvinism, naive individual moral relativism mixed with a dash of professional wrestling, and the ethical decision-making capacities of the producers of *The Jerry Springer Show*.

What does the Starr Report tell us about our moral sensibilities? Perhaps we are adding our own slimy footprints to the mix, while simultaneously we complain about the mess tracked through the house. It is the social polity we are mucking up. John Locke said that people get the government they deserve. I hope he was wrong about that.

We should be as careful of the books we read as company we keep. The dead often have more power than the living.
Tryon Edwards
Jonathan Edwards

Chapter 6

Careful of the
Books We Read

TELLING LIVES

You'll want to know all that David
Copperfield crap, but I don't feel
like going into it.
J.D. Salinger
Catcher in the Rye

My friend, a man barely fifty years old, recently has begun work on an autobiography. He has had a complicated and intriguing life, a tour of duty in Vietnam, a Ph.D. in English literature, and a long and distinguished teaching career. Still, when he told me about the project over lunch recently, I could not hide my wonderment. I thought immediately of a 1930 letter of Bertrand Russell's to his friend, Stanley Unwin. I had read the letter just the evening before in that time when the waking world is the province of newspaper delivery boys and police officers falling in love with the night clerk at the 7-Eleven. Russell told Unwin he feared beginning his autobiography because he might still become the president of Mexico, and the great philosopher and mathematician could not bear to have that left off his self-constructed curriculum vita.

The source of my wonderment and its accompanying skepticism was not, however, the possibility that my friend might go on to do many notable and praiseworthy things in what promises to be the last third of his life. Rather, it was a more philosophical objection.

The self is such a moving target. It is like catching a fly barehanded. I wondered out loud as much about the difficulty of catching it, particularly when the hunter and the hunted are one and the same. Writing a good autobiography presents the problem of getting to know one's subject matter, while simultaneously worrying about who might

123

show up to do the actual writing. Indeed, autobiography may well be the most difficult genre in which to succeed, for there is nothing a person knows less about than himself. So often autobiography is an unrivaled vehicle for telling the truth about a stranger. The mirror we place before us never reveals all that we are. We cannot quickly whirl around to find the backside of ourselves.

There is a second major problem with autobiography, perhaps as insurmountable as the first. For most human beings self-regard has never been enough. We want the regard of certain others. We want them to look at us the way we look at ourselves. We want them to be absorbed and fascinated by the same self that we are. We want the approval of others when we turn ourselves into 300 pages that might nestle on a table at the bedside.

Autobiography, by necessity, begins and ends with John Locke's notion of the self: a continuity of memory over time. But it also involves an inevitable division of the self into the one-who-was and the one-who-is. The one-who-was is at the mercy of the one-who-is. Revenge and self-justification almost always are the fruits borne by the autobiographical tree.

All of us wish to be Huck Finn, at his own funeral, tucked away in the balcony. More than anything, this is what animates autobiography. That we might leave this grand planet and be forgotten like last summer's corn husks urges all of us who put pen to paper to make a record of the particulars of existence. But George Eliot reminds us that most graves go unvisited. Greatness does not always look the same from the outside, nor from the distance of time. Hilare Belloc in *A Conversation With a Cat* suggests that autobiography is like an omelet—there are only two kinds, great and intolerable. I think he was only half right.

First Reading

*Real writers are rarely a comely lot. They
should stick to the page, and leave the acting
to folks who can't write.*
Dorothy Parker
Letters

The reading took place in the foyer of the Martin Luther King
Library, a space with all the open-aired, neoclassical impressiveness
one might expect with the name of an American icon etched in
stone above its wide portals. Three hundred stiff, blue folding chairs
had been arranged on the marble floor. They fanned out impressive-
ly before a raised dais of polished wood. In the middle of that sea of
blue plastic and chrome sat four lonely listeners, as if they had been
thrown together in some terrible nautical accident.

After my introduction, which included my hostess's mention of
the weather (it *was* threatening to rain) as one of the possible reasons
for the sparse attendance, I mounted the dais, my first book in hand,
my first public reading about to begin. I grabbed the podium from
either side, audibly exhaled, and then launched into a reading of my
essays in a voice meant to marry the seriousness of Walter Cronkite
to the timbre of James Earl Jones.

I began with a poignant essay about my father's hands. Four para-
graphs from the end I lost 25% of my audience. He was a short man
with blue running shoes. He walked over to the circulation desk and
in a loud and agitated voice asked why none of the Tom Clancy books
ever seemed to be on the shelves.

The second piece I read was a meditation on examining one's
childhood photographs. Somewhere near the middle of the piece one

of the three remaining members of the audience pulled a brown paper sack from beneath his seat. A moment later he was eating a bologna sandwich. It was later accompanied by chips and a sixteen ounce bottle of soda. Adjusting the volume slightly, I continued with the particulars of my sometimes lonely childhood.

A moment later, a security guard approached the man with the lunch. "You can't eat in here," the guard tried softly.

"What kind of library is this? I thought it was a public library. What's more public than eating?" the man asked, as he crumpled the brown bag into a ball and exited the library.

By my fourth and final essay, an elegiac prose poem about the sea, I had whittled down the audience to the bare minimum: my hostess and a small, well dressed matron. They sat together among a sea of blue folding chairs. The matron stayed until the bitter end, smiling at the appropriate times and, it seemed, appropriately dabbing the corners of her eyes at the most poignant passages.

While packing up my prose, the woman approached. "Excuse me," she said. "Do you mind if I ask you a very personal question?"

"No," I said. "You've sat through this entire reading while fainter hearts had made their escape. I think that alone entitles you to an answer."

"That tie you are wearing," she said evenly, "where did you buy it?"

EMERSON AND THE ESSAY

Emerson is himself a man of occasions, of course,
and he has considered his, and wondered whether
these halls he fills like a thermos will keep his high
hopes hot. He has once again gone to the lectern:
that parlor pulpit and the modest phallus of the teacher.
"I read the other day some verses," he will say, perhaps,
or ask, "Where do we find ourselves?"...and he knows
that he is up to something different and possibly enduring—
a pose his immortality may assume. He is giving definition
to his Being. He is waiting for himself to sail from behind a cloud.

William Gass
Habitations of the Word

The essay is dead, we have been told once again, leaving practitioners of the craft to feel a bit like the sultan's barber who unwittingly
has gone out to buy new scissors as the great man has gone completely bald. Loren Eiseley and E.B. White are dead too—and those
facts clearly have much to do with the supposed demise in this country of a literary form that never quite achieved the respect gained by
its cousins, the short story, the poem, and the sermon.

Ralph Waldo Emerson, the best essayist ever produced in America,
saw the essay as just that, a highly volatile mix, a curious amalgam of
one part first person narrative, one part stirring homily, added to two
parts poetic style and sensibility. I call it a volatile mix because any
essay, at almost any time, is in danger of blowing up on the spot, or
fizzling out like a wet fire cracker or a nervous man left alone with his
girlie magazines at the sexual dysfunction clinic.

Emerson was a failed poet, something that again puts him in the company of Eiseley and White, as well as many of the rest of us who subsequently have chosen the personal essay as our main mode of communication with the reading public, a group not to be confused with the public at large.

Emerson also was a failed preacher, a man who studied at the Harvard Divinity School only to give up his pulpit when persistent doubts about organized religion for a time incapacitated him. It was this doubt that eventually thrust him into the public eye. Indeed, for the next four decades Emerson would make his living and his fame as essayist and public lecturer in a kind of intellectual road show that took him to Europe and throughout the states, including a meeting in 1862 with Abraham Lincoln at the White House.

What made Emerson a fine essayist are the same qualities that marked Montaigne, White, and Eiseley as great practitioners of a genre that Hazlitt wisely called "an ephemeral art, these small gems worthy of an hour's contemplation." Emerson and the others knew that a good essay does not so much explore the topic at hand—in Emerson's case, "Nature," "Friendship," or "Character"—as it does seek to reveal the essayist himself. The ostensible subject of the essay is always the screen on which the essayist projects the real picture, the mind and heart of the writer.

This self-reflective character is what gives the essay its identity, but what provides the essay with power and density is the ability of the reader to recognize himself in the writer's exploration. Emerson says as much in "Master Minds," one of the finest of his short essays:

> What does every earnest man seek in the deep instinct of
> society what but to find himself in another mind. We hail
> with gladness the new acquisition of ourselves.

If the personal essay is dying or dead, this fact perhaps teaches us as much about our contemporary incapacity to read, to follow a complicated argument to its conclusion, to explore a narrative through its beginning, middle, and end. We have lost our ability to be attentive to a fine poem that does not give up its secrets so easily. We no longer are alert to the subtlety of a well-wrought sermon, and if these are the building blocks of the good essay, there should be little wonder why the form is in need of artificial life support.

Emerson lived close to the soul of things, speaking more often like a wild desert mystic or a biblical prophet than a modern man. This sometimes gives one the impression that he wrote all his beautiful sentences and then put them in a hat, randomly picking how they would then appear on the page. If it is true that Emerson was infected with a kind of optimism that most of us cannot manage at the millennium's end, it is equally true that so much of our lives are soulless, so that Emerson, a man preoccupied with the spirit, becomes irrelevant.

If Emerson were alive today, and still possessed of his fine gift of thought, he might raise the question about whether it is the essay that is dying. Perhaps he would urge us to consider again the real subject of the essay: the writer and those around him. He might go on to tell us that the essayist and his art in any literate culture play the part of the canaries kept in nineteenth century mine shafts. Because of their sensitivities the canaries succumbed to pockets of lethal gas long before the miners did. This gave the men time to escape. He would urge us to think about this metaphor while combining his skill as homilist, poet, and spinner of narrative. He was enough of an apocalyptic thinker to wonder if we would heed the warning.

EPIGRAMS

Everything has been said before, but since
nobody listens, we have to keep going back
and beginning all over again.
Andre Gide
Le traite du Narcisse

Anyone can tell the truth, but only a few can make epigrams.
W. Somerset Maugham
A Writer's Notebook

The making of a good epigram is like the construction of a ship in a bottle. It has to be small enough to fit in a tiny space, but it also should come packing a cannon or two. With this in mind, a simple theory always lies behind my employment of an epigram at the head of each of my essays: someone has managed to accomplish in ten or fifteen words what I am about to attempt in 750 to 1,000. If the reader cannot discern my purposes in a particular piece, I always provide an epigram, fully aware that sometimes the coming attractions are better than the feature itself.

The first century Roman writer, Martial, was the inventor of the epigram, and perhaps its finest practitioner. Between the ages of forty-five and sixty he composed twelve volumes of epigrams, over 8,000 entries. When honored by a friend for the brevity of a particular epigram, Martial commented, "You dear friend have written nothing, so your epigrams are still smaller than my best."

The German philosopher and philologist Friedrich Nietzsche wrote marvelous epigrams. They were usually so good, he didn't bother to provide the essays that might have followed them.

Consider, for example this *bon mot* on sadness: "Men of profound sadness betray themselves when they are happy: they have a way of embracing happiness as if they wanted to crush it." In his *Twilight of the Idols*, Nietzsche suggests that his ambition is to say in a few sentences what other men say in whole books—or what other men do not say in whole books.

Oscar Levant defined an epigram as "a wisecrack that played Carnegie Hall," and H.L. Mencken in *A Book of Burlesques* called it "a platitude with vine leaves in its hair." But both men might have been quicker to point out that they were making an exception to their epigrams about epigrams, thus avoiding the perilous dangers of a self-referential paradox.

The epigram is not like any other literary form. For one thing, there is no such thing as a bad epigram. If it is not short, it is a paragraph, and not an epigram. If it does not have punch to it, then it is a platitude. Epigrams are like most other simple but useful inventions: the rest of us are sorry we did not think of it first.

The real devotee of the epigrammatic form is more like a prospector than anything else. Using a book of quotations for finding an epigram is like a '49er walking into a jewelry store to find gold. Using *Bartlett's* has all the suspense and requires all the skill that Ahab would need to find a whale at SeaWorld.

In our own time, it is difficult to find a good practitioner of the epigram. In my parents' generation Winston Churchill and Adlai Stevenson were always good for an epigram or two. But more recently, the epigram has fallen on hard times, replaced by the sound-byte. Sound-bytes should not be confused with epigrams; it's not only possible, it is likely that any given sound-byte is a bad one.

Failed sound-bytes bear the same relationship to epigrams that anti-matter has to matter. Failed sound-bytes are really anti-epigrams. George Bush was, perhaps, the inventor of the anti-epigram, where wit and brevity could not be found within hollering distance of each other. Robert Dole is the most recent practitioner of the anti-epigram. If William Hazlitt was correct that "epigrams tell all at once, or not at all," then it is clear that Mr. Dole has chosen the latter.

A Magical House

Old houses don't belong to people,
the people belong to the houses.
Gladys Taber
Still Meadows Daybook

Every house is a hospital.
Henry David Thoreau
Letters

There are particular places that tell human beings what ought to happen there. They whisper incessantly until we get the message: certain dark gardens with trellises and old stone walls cry out for a good murder; particular Victorian houses in slight disrepair demand to be haunted; and certain craggy coastlines, from the beginning, are set apart to accommodate shipwrecks.

I have lived in this old house now for only a year. Since the day I arrived it has informed me clearly, almost rudely at times, that a writer ought to live here. In the early morning the sun invades my small study with shafts of golden light worthy of Goethe's poetry: "colors are the deeds and sufferings of light." In autumn, the oaks stubbornly cling to leaves long past dead. They whisper for something, perhaps a eulogy, before they are willing to give up the fruits of their labor.

In winter, in the dead of night, the heating system hisses and groans, forcing air through the pipes and my spirit to return from among the sleeping and the dead. This house makes demands on those it awakens. And so, I arise, turn on the desk lamp, and for a few minutes the practical jostles with the limitless until the eternal wins. I dutifully begin to follow the house's instructions. Something is to be written here on this night.

The house has awakened me on this still evening—an evening with no wind and a spill of stars bright enough to convince me that there is a God out there somewhere— to remind me that the busiest of living agents are often the thoughts of certain dead people. I was awakened by a line from one of Jane Austen's letters read earlier in the evening. She points out to a grieving friend that one does not love a place less for having suffered in it. She speaks wisely of the curious affection we humans seem to have for the places where our lives have met with great pain. She writes about sorrow mingling with the wall-paper so that one's personal history becomes inextricably bound to the character of the house in which it is lived.

Now, just a moment ago, there came clanging and hissing through the pipes, like language from another world, a line from the *Confessions*, where St. Augustine wonders why we cry at the theater and then find it supremely pleasurable. These single ideas supplied by Austen and Augustine chase each other for several hours, until an essay is born of their union. These lives—the fifth century church-man and the Victorian novelist—were separated by 1500 years, more than 75% of the entire Christian calendar. And yet, they now mingle on the page, in a kind of marriage of the mind, brought together by a man to whom neither had been properly introduced.

This is a magical house.

The Writing Life

For several days after my first book was published
I carried it about in my pocket, and took surreptitious
peeps at it to make sure the ink had not faded.

J.M. Barrie
A Reader for Writers

Samuel Johnson thought there was only one reason for the serious writer to ever take up the pen: money. All other loftier sentiments about the motivation of the writer, he believed, are lies, or at the very least half-truths, which are nothing more than lies wearing an expensive suit coat without the matching trousers.

For twenty-three springs I have identified myself as "writer/teacher" on my federal income tax forms. But I never have made more than $4,000 in a single year of pushing the pen. I suppose this is a bit like identifying one's place of business as "gourmet restaurant/convenience store" when you have only one small table in the back placed among the beef jerky, potato chips, and the big gulp machine.

Perhaps if I were to make as much money as Dr. Johnson or Danielle Steele, I would think differently about why I write, and, by extension, for whom I write. But as it is, I have definite ideas about why I do it, despite the fact that I never seem to do enough of it, nor do I ever get paid enough for what I have done.

I write because I can't keep from writing—the way a gnat must plaster itself against a bare light bulb on a sultry summer evening. Writing, like breathing, is not something in my conscious control. If I did not do it, surely I would die. Writing happens to me, like falling in love or being in an automobile accident. It is more like being struck by lightning than it is like baking a cake.

I write when the whole of life is decidedly unbearable, or when joy has become so much a part of the fabric of things that I must tell someone immediately. Putting it on the printed page has the added advantage of the writer not having to be around when the telling is finished.

Although the fact I write is not a conscious choice, where I write most certainly is. I have chosen to write in Maryland, as many others have: Poe, Mencken, Fitzgerald, Stephen Dixon, Anne Tyler, Madison Bell, and the exquisite poet and short story maker, Josephine Jacobsen, for all of her nearly nine decades on the planet.

I write in Maryland because I can look out my window and watch things change. We have four real seasons here, and nature is as good a place to look as any when the writer gets bored with himself. The natural world is so good at reinventing itself, something the writer must learn to do if the spigot is not prematurely to be shut off.

I write in Maryland because I grew up here and because my college remedial English composition teacher told me the writer should only write about the things he knows. Like the natural world, what I know seems constantly to change.

I write here because so many of the people and places I love are found in this state. I write in Maryland because of the Maryland Room of the Pratt Library; I write here because of the painted screens in East Baltimore. I write here because the crabs are better than anywhere else, and the baseball has been so good for so long.

But mostly I write here because I can't imagine living and writing anywhere else.

*Father in Heaven, when the thought
of you wakes in our hearts, let it not awaken
like a frightened bird that flies away in dismay,
but like a child waking from a deep sleep
with a heavenly smile.*
Soren Kierkegaard
Journals

Chapter 7

A Child with a
Heavenly Smile

Good Trees

*There is an endless yawning difference
between God and man, and hence in the
situation of contemporaneousness, to
become a Christian is to be transformed into
the likeness of God. This becomes an even
greater human torment, and hence also a
crime in the eyes of one's neighbor.*
Soren Kierkegaard
The Training in Christianity

*The notion of a tree or plant, the fruit of
which would sustain life indefinitely, was
widespread in the ancient Near East.*
Harry Hunt
The Dictionary of the Bible

On the inside, it did not look much like a church. The room resembled—in shape and atmosphere—a fair-sized auditorium. Several
hundred fixed seats were arranged in a semi-circle. All the seats
were occupied by young men and women, with a sprinkling of
elderly people and some mostly impatient children. The focus of the
room was a raised square-shaped dais, little more than a slightly
raised platform really. In the middle of the platform was a large,
wood-grain podium. Atop the podium rested a well-thumbed, rather
ornate red and gold-edge copy of the King James Version of the
bible. Behind the podium stood the preacher, silver-haired, distinguished looking, about fifty. He wore a black Doctor of Ministry robe

with three blue velvet bars on each sleeve. He waited for his cue from the soundman.

Behind the preacher, to the rear of the platform, could be seen a large cross made of a dark wood that matched the podium. On the cross hung the waxen, life-size figure of a thin man about thirty years old. The figure was unclad, save for a loin cloth. There was a deep wound visible in his left side, just below his protruding rib-cage. The head, which wore a crown of thorns, was slightly tilted to the left, the chin resting on his chest.

When the preacher was given the signal by a tall man in the sound booth, his voice carried a great distance. It was not the microphone. His ability at projection had some other source. It was as if the man carried within his breast his own amplification system.

"I want to speak to you this morning...indeed Jesus wishes me to speak with you this morning...about how a good tree cannot bear bad fruit."

When the man pronounced the word "Jesus" it was in three syllables. He gave the word a peculiar drawn out sound like a tea kettle beginning to boil, or the air slowly escaping from a bad tire.

"You know my dear friends," the preacher said, "a good tree cannot bear bad fruit. And a bad tree cannot bear good fruit. And just as trees are known by the fruits they bear, so too people...all people...in the end time are to be judged by their actions."

While the preacher was in the process of delivering these lines, behind him, the body on the cross mysteriously came to life. At first, he did little more than painfully lift his head, eyes fluttering, adjusting to the light, as he began to listen to the homily in progress. The woman behind camera three thought she was seeing things. Some others thought it was done with special effects.

"That Judge, you know, will not be of this world...No...That judge is an eternal judge, an omniscient Judge, a judge of the living and a judge of the dead."

Now, behind him, the man on the cross frantically had begun to pull at his right hand, he tensed his arm as far as he could, attempting to free the hand completely from the cross piece. The director looked nervously at the men in the glass booth behind the congregation. A nervous titter began to make its way through the crowd.

"We must remember," the preacher said confidently, " Jesus cursed the fig tree. And why did he do that? Why should Jesus bother to curse this fig tree in chapter eleven of Saint Mark's gospel?" While dabbing perspiration from his forehead, the preacher stared for a moment at the appropriate text.

"Why?...why did Jesus curse the fig tree?...because...because it bore no fruit."

By now, the body on the cross had managed to free his right hand. For the briefest of moments the man stared incredulously at the bloody hole in his palm. A woman in the first row coughed; a small child with shinny black shoes that swung beneath her seat whined that she wanted to go home. But most of the others sat silent, transfixed by the scene unfolding before them.

"If we are to be judged as righteous, we must bear good fruit. And it cannot be just any ol' good fruit, it must also be the fruit for which we were intended. Apple trees don't bear oranges; you can't get cherries from a peach tree; and you won't find any plums growing on a pear tree. We must bear good fruit, but it must be the fruit that God has planted in each and every one of us. We must bear that fruit which God's providence has planted in each of us."

The man on the cross now began painfully to reach with his free hand at the left hand still attached to the cross piece. He pulled frantically at the second and middle fingers, working at this for several minutes, only stopping to catch his breath and to wipe his brow with the free hand.

"And so, my dear friends..."

Out of the corner of his right eye, the preacher—staring sideways in the way the astronomers suggest one ought to watch an eclipse—realized something behind him was greatly amiss. And, in a single motion, he picked up an industrial-size staple gun from the hidden shelf of the podium and whirled around, his robes flowing like the feathers of a giant bird, to meet the body on the cross, his left hand striking the man forcefully in the chest. And in that same moment, the man on the cross, who had managed to free his second hand, was thrown back against the cross, his head hitting the upright with a thud, his arms splayed back to their original position.

Bam...Bam... the noise of the stapling carried even farther than the preacher's voice. The older man had stapled the struggling figure securely back to the cross. Then, in the same tone he had employed before the interruption, the preacher continued:

"And so my dear friends, we must remember that the day will come, we know not what day, when we will be judged by the fruits we have borne. Will you be prepared when that day comes?...will you be prepared?" The preacher pointed at some children behind him; the body struggled for a moment longer. Some ladies in the first few rows thought he might have mumbled something. Then the man collapsed, as his head, slightly tilted to the left, came once again to rest on his chest.

"Just as trees are known by the fruit they bear, people...all people my brothers and sisters...are known by their actions."

When the preacher nodded a moment later, the blue-robed choir broke into a stirring hymn. For the remainder of the hour, the camera crew avoided showing the man on the cross. Later, the Television Ministries Network, the sponsors of the program, received several phone calls from concerned viewers that the homily had frightened their children. The following week, the preacher used a plain wooden cross as backdrop for his sermon.

No complaints were received.

Looking For Eros

*It is the fate of sensual love to become
extinguished when it is satisfied; for it to
be able to last, it must be mixed with
purely tender components.*

Sigmund Freud
*Group Psychology and the
Analysis of the Ego*

*I had discovered that Love might be a
pastime as well as a tragedy. I gave myself
to it with pagan innocence.*

Isadora Duncan
My Life

Rarely do the gods meet in full assembly, by their natures they tend to be loners. When they do, it is usually for a particularly vexing issue, one that requires more than one celestial mind to think it through. Most of the older gods could only remember a time or two—Prometheus stealing fire, Orpheus finding Eurydice— that they were ever called together. It happened only in the most dire of circumstances.

On this morning, Eros stood before the assembly. He was tired and cranky. He had that kind of look in his immortal eyes the gods get when they have gone a long time without the proper celestial sleep. Eros was a hunted god, and members of the pathetic human race were his stalkers.

When Zeus asked why the young god now stood before the Immortals, Eros launched rather quickly into an impassioned analysis of the problem. He was being pursued by all manner of human beings—by priests and paupers, kings and clerks, believers and apostates alike. No longer did Eros need to use his bow and magic arrows, never again would human beings fall to his stealth and cunning. Now he was the prey, pursued at every turn by hapless humans who desired what they thought only he could give them. Whatever continent he roamed, they found him. He had tried hiding in the most inconspicuous of places, but wherever he found himself, only a few steps behind were these pathetic mortals each searching desperately for him. Then he tried a kind of divine reverse psychology, conspicuous places: wallets and pocketbooks; massage parlors and libraries; in well worn copies of the *Kama Sutra*, Masters and Johnson, and the books of Henry Miller. But wherever he hid, the pesky and loathsome human beings soon found him.

It took several minutes for Eros to tell his story of woe to the assembled Immortals. He spoke in a clear and steady voice, but a voice that at times failed to mask the passion brought on by his predicament. Some of the older gods whispered to each other that the young god needed to get a hold of himself, what the gods sometimes called a "celestial grip." Eros told the assembled Immortals that he had tried temples, markets, brothels, and monasteries alike, but wherever he tried to hide, the humans would find him. For a while, in what at first he thought was a brilliant plan, Eros tried hiding in a pill called Viagra, but it did not work out the way he had planned.

After Eros finished his story, the gods in turn did lots of thinking out loud. Some opined that this was just the excuse they needed for eliminating the pesky humans once and for all. Others suggested that it might be a good idea to turn all of humanity into donkeys. Still others made less violent suggestions, but all spoke with the kind of loud volume and nervous agitation the gods only reserved for moments when in their hearts they feared they were not making much sense.

The discussion continued for days, one god after another making suggestions that seemed silly to Eros, and to all but each of the speakers in his turn. The gods in assembly had been stumped. It so rarely happened this way. It was not since the riddles of Zeno that they all had performed so poorly.

The gods are a race of beings who worry most about what others of their kind think about them. None of the gods wished to appear stupid before the others. This, of course, is precisely what happened. For the next several days, each of the gods in his turn made one ridiculous suggestion after another, one more preposterous than the next, until finally, all the gods were as exhausted and as demoralized as Eros himself.

Eros glanced out over the many deities assembled on Olympus, the tops of white, puffy cumulus clouds encircling the top of the mountain. Eros thought about how exhausting and unproductive the gods' posturing had been. Finally, he had a flash of divine insight—the solution had been there all along. A moment later Eros began to describe his new plan. He would hide deep in the hearts of every human being. None would think to look for him there.

This is what he did. And that is why it is a rare day when any human being finds him.

LEARNING TO PRAY

Prayer always has an effect, even
if it is not the effect we desire.
Alexis Carrel
Reflections on Life

The wish to pray is a prayer in itself.
George Bernanos
The Diary of a Country Priest

From his chair on the ship's observation deck all the bishop could see were sky meeting sea and sea meeting sky. The voyage had, at least so far, been a smooth one—the wind favorable, the weather fair. When the bishop left his chair to stretch his legs, he encountered a group of tourists, standing near the prow, listening to an old sailor with eyes the translucent color of the green sea.

The old man was telling his impromptu audience something, as he pointed out to the sea glistening in the sunshine. When the bishop drew nearer the sailor stopped in mid-sentence, took off his cap, and stared at the polished rivets in the deck.

"Don't let me disturb you," the bishop said smoothly. "I have come to listen like the others, please continue your tale."

"He was telling us about the hermits," said a small round woman with a camera.

"What hermits are they?" the bishop asked as he squinted out at the flat sea that seemed to trade subtle shades of gray with the sky above it.

"The small island, you can see it over there," the sailor said looking up. He pointed to a spot ahead and slightly to the left of the ship. "That is the island where the holy men live."

"Where is the island, I don't see it?" the bishop inquired, squinting out again at what, at least to him, seemed nothing more than an infinite variation of gray.

"Do you see the small white cloud, the one shaped like a fish. It is there, to the left."

The bishop looked carefully but he could not see the island. Again he squinted for a long time until finally he turned to the sailor, only half believing what the old man had said.

"They are very holy men, your excellency. They have lived there for many years. When I was a cabin boy, now more than fifty years ago, the older sailors would point out the island, and tell the story...though, you understand...I never have been there myself."

The bishop looked again and now he could see a dark streak just below the horizon, though he still was not sure there was something there.

Later, in the evening at dinner, the bishop asked the captain about the island. "So it is said," offered the captain, a man with unusually long limbs and the bearing of a military commander. "Fisherman and old sailors say that three ancient hermits inhabit the island. They say the men have been there for longer than either of us have been alive. They say the holy men pray for the salvation of our souls...that they have a very special relationship with God...I don't know if it is true. You know, your excellency, there are many tales told at sea."

"I should like to go there to see if the holy men exist," said the bishop. "Could we manage it somehow? If it is not too much trouble, might I go in the morning?"

The captain tried to dissuade the bishop, but the cleric was insistent in a way that only the clergy and the military fully understand. And so, in the morning a comfortable chair for the bishop was placed at the prow of a small row boat, and within half an hour the boat with its four young oarsmen had moved within plain view of the tiny island. And there, among the waves, stood three small men with long yellowing beards. They were shoeless and wore course brown tunics with hemp gathered tightly at the waist. In a few more minutes of rowing, the small boat glided to a stop on the island.

When the bishop stepped out of the boat, the three men instinctively bowed to him. As he gave them his blessing, they bowed still lower. "I have heard," said the bishop solemnly, "that you are very holy men, and that you pray for the salvation of souls. Please, show me, one of God's humble servants, how you pray."

For a moment the three looked at each other, in a way that suggested they were touched by fever. Finally, the oldest and smallest of the hermits sunk to his knees in the sand. Immediately his brothers followed, and together they began to pray, looking to the heavens.

"You are three, we are three, all about is harmony. Amen."

They repeated the line in unison another dozen times, never once taking their eyes off a cloud that looked vaguely like a giant leviathan.

Presently, the bishop, with a bemused look, helped the oldest of the hermits to his feet. "God has sent me to teach you to pray," the bishop said soothingly. "I will teach you to pray the way Jesus at the last supper taught his disciples."

For the next eight hours, the bishop tenderly and painstakingly taught the three ancient hermits the Lord's Prayer. But it was not an easy task. The first old ascetic had a habit, after a few hours, of leaving out the part about "Thy will be done." The second had trouble remembering "Now and at the hour of our death," and the third man, the tallest of the three, could not seem to get right "Give us this day our daily bread." The four oarsmen had fallen asleep farther up the shore and by late afternoon they had received a nasty burn from the tropical sun.

Still the bishop patiently continued until shadows from the tallest trees of the island began creeping over the shore where they had established the impromptu catechetical class. Finally, all three hermits seem to get it right, as the captain with his bull-horn announced that they had best weigh anchor, and the young oarsmen quickly jumped to their feet.

When the bishop returned to the ship, he had his seat placed at the stern so he could watch the island receding in the distance. He thought about his years as a missionary, a time when, as a young priest, he had taught thousands to pray. He thought about the many catechetical classes where he had instructed children and adults all hungry to pray as the Lord had prayed. But the bishop also reflected that he had never before taught an older nor an odder group of students.

As the full moon light sparkled on the surface of the water, the bishop thought he saw a great light in the distance. "There must be a boat sailing after us," he thought.

A moment later he could see that it was not one light, but three. The thin hermits, their beards flapping in the spray, were running on the surface of the water. All three men sprinted along, as if an invisible road had been spread before them, just below the surface of the water. As they ran, the arms of the hermits gesticulated wildly, an iridescent quality accompanying the movement of every limb.

In a moment the three had reached the ship, each wheezing in exactly the way one might expect. After a good bit of coughing, the three spoke in unison: "Your excellency, already we have forgotten the words of your magnificent prayer. Please, before you return, you must teach it to us again. We are old, and our memories have gone bad, and we do not wish to be deprived of so beautiful a prayer."

And with these words, the three holy men knelt expectantly on the open sea.

THE MYSTERIOUS MUSTARD 'TREE'

I never knew how soothing trees are, many trees
spreading gracefully, like the presence of God.

D.H. Lawrence
Letters

God is much more a verb than a noun.

Soren Kierkegaard
Journals

The tale of the mustard seed, a familiar gospel story from the New Testament, presents us with a bit of a paradox. The story is clear enough: within a series of related parables, Jesus spins the tale of a grain of mustard, which, when planted in the soil, is the smallest of all the earth's seeds. Once it is sown, however, it springs up to become a giant shrub (or even "tree" as the Greek suggests) with branches big enough for the birds to build their nests in. At first, the moral of the tale seems clear enough, so clear that the writer of Mark's gospel does not even bother to tell us what it means. Indeed, he chooses instead to end the narrative by saying, "By means of many such parables he taught them the message in a way they could understand. To them he spoke only by way of parable, while he kept explaining things privately to his disciples."

This parable long has been a favorite in the English speaking world. It generally has been employed to make the point that momentous things may come from small beginnings, or that the most profound and thorough of changes often begins simply and silently. Thomas Carlyle uses the story in an essay on "Boswell's Life of Johnson," to describe the fertility and power of Johnson's prose, despite its brevity. Thomas Hardy quotes from the parable for similar purposes in *Far from the Madding Crowd*. Alexander Anderson in his biography of Aldous Huxley comments that from a single idea Huxley so frequently made vast foliage, "like the biblical seed of mustard sprouting into lodging for the fowl of the air."

Although we seem to have made much use of this story, the tale leaves us with a number of odd facts, many of them botanical. First, carrot seeds are much smaller than mustard seeds, and so are many others. The orchard seed, a plant known to any Palestinian farmer of the first century, is half the size of the mustard seed. Indeed, the tiny orchard seed is not much bigger than the period at the end of this sentence. Thus, the title "the smallest of the earth's seeds" should not be bestowed on the mustard, but on the much more impressive flowering orchard that manages to grow from a speck of a seed.

A second oddity about the parable is that the *Brassica nigra* and the *Sinapsis nigra*, the two most common varieties of mustard plant in the ancient Middle-East, even with a good diet of modern Miracle-Gro, and an inordinate amount of tender care, would grow only to four feet in height, certainly never large enough to be called a "tree." The mustard plant does not grow to an impressive size, for it is an annual. Although it does grow very rapidly, it would never be suitable for nesting birds, unless the birds in question were of the humming variety, and thus saw the diminutive mustard seed as a mouthful.

So what are we to make of this story? Perhaps we should simply point out that Jesus was a carpenter, not a farmer. Maybe we should say flora and fauna were not his specialty, and leave it at that? I think not, for this is no ordinary mustard plant. One gets the nagging feeling that something much more is going on beneath the surface of this narrative, a tale about a misdescribed seed that grows to an improbable height, so that fictitious birds might make their nonexistent nests there.

Our story is made all the more complicated when we understand that chapter four of Mark, sometimes called the "parable chapter" by biblical scholars, is one of only two long speeches that Jesus gives in all of that gospel. The other long discourse from the mouth of Jesus comes in chapter thirteen of Mark. Both speeches are primarily about eschatology, and undoubtedly are related. Chapter four combines the series of seed parables to explain why the proclamation of God's reign is meeting with resistance. It is also designed to insure the audience that despite the present hardship and lack of progress, God's reign eventually will burst forth with amazing fecundity. Much of chapter thirteen is taken up with the description of that reign.

This explanation is good as far as it goes, but it does not explain why this improbable tree will be able to support the birds of the air on its branches. For some intriguing hints at an answer, we might do well to turn to the Hebrew bible. The fourth chapter of the Old Testament's book of Daniel portrays the Babylonian empire as a large tree in which the nations of the world roost like birds. The same image is used in several places in the ancient world to describe the extent of the Assyria empire at its height.

In the seventeenth chapter of Ezekiel, the sixth century prophet attempts to describe the messianic kingdom that will replace the humiliation of the exile. He chooses this same image of a renewed Israel as a giant tree in which birds might reside. In all these Old Testament allusions, the emphasis in the image of the great tree holding up the birds' nests is one of physical strength and military power. They are snapshots of nations flexing their muscles, both real and imagined. They are images of brute force, the by-product of physical power or its threat. Could it be that we are supposed to understand the story of the improbable mustard plant in light of these earlier references? I think so.

Unlike these Old Testament images, the kingdom to be brought to fruition in the gospels is based on love. Its authority and authenticity come from love, not from power. At first blush, a kingdom or a company, a family or a friendship built on love may well not look like much of an edifice, particularly when compared to one built on money or power. But a family or friendship based on love, the kind that Jesus exhorts us in the gospels to embrace, is one with sturdy branches—what may seem to the outsider to be improbably sturdy ones. The secret to the mysterious sturdiness of these branches is to be found in their roots, in God Himself.

This realization brings us to another biblical seed tale in which we find the origins of the sturdiness of our improbably sturdy mustard plant, a faith that today continues to hold all the nations of the world. In the first seed story Jesus tells the crowd how a man scatters seeds on the ground. He goes to bed and gets up day after day. Through it all the seed silently sprouts and grows without the man knowing how it happens. God's mustard tree is the result of what God does, not the independent actions of human beings. All the farmer has done is sown the seed, everything else is outside his control. In the drama of history, God is the primary actor. Beneath the improbable mustard seed holding up the entire world are the roots, the creator God.

If God is the ground of our improbable mustard "tree," then Jesus is the paradoxical tree itself. A God/Man, a walking, breathing paradox, improbably tacked up on a wooden cross, his arms spread like the boughs of a tree, so that he might save the rest of us. He displayed his authority precisely by refusing to show his physical power. This is why Jesus looked no more like a god than the lowly mustard bush resembled that improbable-but-great tree it blossomed into. Certainly a cross would appear to be an unlikely place on which the nations of the world might build their nests. But they did.

The man suffering on the cross did not look like a god, but then we couldn't see his roots.

On Prayer

*An angel collects all the prayers offered
in synagogues, weaves them into a garland
and places them on God's head.*
The Zohar 21.4

*He...folded his large brown hands across
his chest, uplifted his closed eyes, and offered
a prayer so deeply devout that he
seemed kneeling and praying at the bottom of the sea.*
Herman Melville
Moby Dick

The metaphysics and epistemology of prayer long has occupied my imagination. As early as the second grade, while waiting patiently beneath my wrought-iron and wooden desk for the end of atomic bomb practice, or simply for the end, I have learned to pray in some of the oddest places for some of the strangest things.

While playing football on a particularly bad high school team I remember having two strategies about prayer. If the other team was from a public school, I prayed that we would win, reasoning, of course, that having some tangential relationship to the saints, the martyrs, and the pope, we would have an edge with a few well-placed prayers before the game. When we competed against a fellow Catholic high school, however, I counted up the players on the other team. If they had more than we did, I did not raise my petitions for victory; instead I prayed I would not get hurt. I am not sure what this has to do with the fact that I had an injury-plagued high school athletic career.

These days my thoughts about prayer are more complicated, and not nearly so utilitarian. I have been thinking quite a bit lately about the relationship of prayer to despair. George Eliot came closest to the nature of despair when she called it "the painful eagerness of unfed hope." I have come only recently to understand that it is through prayer that hope is most nourishingly fed. Prayer is not a sign of despair, it is a response to it. It is not what one does when it is time to give up; it is what one should do when it is time to get started.

Many of my friends see the efficacy of prayer as nonsense. They say it is like throwing straw to a drowning man. It is probably true that a single piece of straw has never saved a drowning man, but I do know that sometimes the mere glance at a single piece of floating straw is enough to make despair pause, if for only a moment. Sometimes that is enough.

Some believers and cynics alike see prayer as a substitute for work, when it is primarily a way of exposing oneself to the promptings of God. One does not pray in place of work, rather it is the effort to work further and to be efficient beyond the range of one's normal powers.

Long ago William James pointed out the therapeutic advantages of prayer, even, he said, if it turns out that no one is listening. Prayer finds a place to put rage, the one emotion that always comes, uninvited, creeping and crawling into life. Prayer is the only form of revolt that ever makes anger stand upright and answer for itself.

More than anything, prayer is an act of daring, and thus, like other courageous acts, it is a difficult thing to do. It is no easier to pray than it is to create a great work of music or write a fine poem; it might be more difficult than building a bridge, or discovering a scientific truth. Healing the sick or fully understanding another human being probably are more difficult, though, because they require daring, they seem so much like praying that it is not easy to say.

Above all, prayer revives the heart the way a bit of wind and incense revive a small coal. This, of course, is one reason why we never think to pray for our enemies. It is only the dying who contemplate such a thing. The dying, like the dead, always seem so much closer to the center of things.

THE ANATOMY OF HYPOCRISY

Hypocrite (n.) one who, professing virtue that he does not respect, secures the advantage of seeming to be what he despises.

Ambrose Bierce
The Devil's Dictionary

Hypocrisy is the homage that vice pays to virtue.

Francois La Rochefoucauld
Maxims, no. 28

There are few gospel narratives as transparently clear as the twenty-third chapter of Matthew. Speaking of the scribes and Pharisees Jesus tells us, "Their words are bold, but their deeds are few," and "All their works are performed to be seen." The subject at hand is hypocrisy, and Jesus gives us a thoughtful lesson on its anatomy in just twelve short verses. Indeed, although the Pharisaic movement was one of the four respected and competing religious and political ideologies of first century Palestine, the Galilean's portrait is such a vivid one that in the western world the word "Pharisee" has come to be synonymous with "hypocrite."

There is, of course, a major danger in talking about hypocrisy—particularly from the pulpit. One runs the risk of sounding exactly like those one wishes to call to task. There are many reasons that hypocrisy is dangerous. One is that the hypocrite, because of his capacity for self-deception, is often the last to know about his hypocrisy. If there is one thing a hypocrite hates, it is hypocrisy. Sometimes falsehoods are not uttered, they are lived.

These days one would have to have a character like Jesus' to emerge unscathed from talking about hypocrisy. Perhaps because so many of us take it as a regular part of the moral landscape. We have come to expect hypocrisy in so many parts of life: in politics, among lawyers, in our sports heroes, and sadly, even among the clergy, that we often take a stance toward these groups that roughly resembles the attitude we might have had for a shady used car salesman a few decades ago.

When we do see genuinely good people these days, we often wonder about what is wrong with them. We sometimes assume they are hypocrites because many of our regular encounters with people turn out that way. It is as if we have come to expect hypocrisy among our leaders, be they religious or secular.

It would be no exaggeration to say we live in an age of hypocrisy. It might be wise, then, for the thoughtful homilist to escape with as little commentary as possible, lest one make the same kind of mistake, peculiar to our age, made by Anglican Archbishop Ullathorne a few years ago. While the bishop was lecturing on humility an eager student interrupted the famous cleric in mid-sentence: "Your Grace, excuse me, but could you tell me, what is the best book on humility?"

The bishop replied without hesitation: "There is but one truly good contemporary book on humility. I wrote it myself." Witnesses at the lecture attest that he talked for another forty minutes on the subject at hand.

The Psalmist speaks of a "heart, not proud / nor eyes haughty," while Malachai talks of "laying virtue to the heart." For the ancient Jews, the heart was far more than a complicated pump. It was for them the seat of emotions, as well as the center of the intellect. It was the organ of thinking and feeling.

For the ancient Hebrew people, the heart was the place where both hypocrisy and its opposite, humility, are born. The prophet Malachai and the writer of Psalm 131 understood that there is some virtue in almost every vice, except hypocrisy. They both appreciated as well the greatest irony in the practice of hypocrisy: although it attempts to make a secret mockery of virtue, hypocrisy pays a kind of compliment to it. The hypocrite unfailingly shows the way we ought to be.

It is fitting, then, that these two texts from the Old Testament are joined with a New Testament gospel passage to give us a fuller picture of the nature and uses of hypocrisy. Indeed, Jesus spends the first half of the twenty-third chapter of Matthew delineating the anatomy of hypocrisy. It amounts to building a public self that is significantly better than the one who actually inhabits the soul. Hypocrisy is a complex sin, for it amounts to bearing false witness against oneself; it is a curious coveting of one's neighbor's character, rather than his goods. Above all, hypocrisy always involves murdering the truth.

If the first several verses of this gospel from Matthew teach us about the nature of hypocrisy, in the end of the pericope Jesus offers some practical advice on avoiding the hypocrite label for oneself. That advice culminates in the line: "The greatest among you will be the one who serves the rest."

There is, of course, no sounder advice for avoiding hypocrisy, for as Jesus points out, the hypocrite always asks more of others than he does of himself. Jesus seems to be suggesting that if we can make an honest effort to "serve the rest," and forget for a while about the self, then we might avoid this most common form of hypocrisy.

But there is also a more subtle form of hypocrisy with which to contend. It is the kind of hypocrisy I imagine Jesus struggling with in the Garden of Gethsemane. After one has "served the rest" and achieved an authentic kind of humility, there is the added danger that one might become too proud of one's feat. Humility is hard earned, but if we take it too seriously, it disappears and is instantly replaced by this most subtle form of hypocrisy, the kind that T.S. Eliot seems to have struggled over in writing *Murder in the Cathedral*. There Archbishop Thomas á Beckett warns us: "The last temptation is the greatest treason, to do the right thing for the wrong reason." Marcus Aurelius reminds us in his second century *Meditations* that "[n]othing is more scandalous than a man who is proud of his humility."

Real humility presents us with a curious paradox: in order to possess it, one must not take it too seriously. Perhaps this is why even Jesus commends his spirit to the Father as his last action from the cross. This is also why Paul speaks of himself as a "libation poured out." The truly humble know it is always best to put things in God's hands.

All of these observations lead us to a final paradox of Christianity, one that could easily merit a homily of its own: Christianity is a religion whose founder consistently preached a gospel of genuine humility, and yet the Christian tradition so often has bred more proud, stubborn, and self-absorbed types than any other religion. It is no wonder that today the word "Christian," in some circles, has become a synonym for "Pharisee." It is hardly what Jesus had in mind.

The Existence of Other Minds

Change rests simply upon a word.
It is a mere name.
Shankara
Advaita

What an absurd amount of energy I
have been wasting all my life trying to
figure out how things "really are," when
all the time they weren't.
Hugh Prather
Notes to Myself

The two monks made their way along the narrow path in the darkness. They followed the twisting foot path from their mud hut, through the forest, and down to the narrow road leading to the river. Although the rule about silence had been in effect for many years, the two men were not slaves to it. Thus it was their habit to talk quietly as they made their way to the bridge leading to the monastery, to morning prayers, and then another day of heavy labor. Their quiet conversations ranged over a sometimes odd and wide collection of topics, things that many of the older monks in the monastery surely would frown upon were they to know about these clandestine conversations. And so, each morning, upon crossing the bridge, they followed the rules more strictly.

On most days, by habit, coincidence, or perhaps by some other way, the monks arrived at the bridge just as the upper rim of the sun made its appearance over the mountains to the East. It was usually an extraordinary sight: deeper purples and saffron than the colors of their faded robes. The colors seemed to spread over the tops of the mountains as if liquid was being poured from the heavens. The sight of daybreak from the bridge was the kind of experience that might occupy their imaginations for the remainder of the day had the concentration required for proper prayer, and then the sheer difficulty of their work in the fields, not demanded their full attention.

On one particular morning upon their arrival at the bridge, the river Po was running swiftly. It had rained the previous night, and as they made their way to morning prayers the two monks had worried about their crops, which lined the dirt road on the far side of the bridge leading to the monastery. For a short time, their quiet conversation had centered on a rumor the younger monk had heard that if they could not salvage part of the soy crop, the monastery would close. But by the time they arrived at the bridge, the monks' attention had turned to other things.

Looking over the railing at a small pool which had formed by the river bank in the protection of some smooth brown stones, Bin Tu, the older of the two monks, said, almost in a whisper, "Look how the minnows are darting. The fish certainly are enjoying themselves this morning."

Tzi Tien, the younger man, just elevated to the status of monk a year earlier, until now had been looking intently at his companion. Then he leaned out over the railing and stared at the minnows.

"The fish dart this way every morning," he said, straightening himself up. "For months we have made this trip together and you have just come to notice them now. Besides, you are not a fish, and thus how do you know if the fish are enjoying themselves or not?"

Again Bin Tu whispered his reply: "My friend, you are not I—how do you know that I do not know what brings pleasure to these fish. Indeed, how do you know that I am not now having the same thoughts as these fish?"

Tzi Tien thought for a moment, by then the sun had made its full appearance. Then he said this, "If because I am not you, I cannot not know whether you know what it is that brings pleasure to these fish, then it must also be the case that because you are not a fish, then you cannot know what gives pleasure to these fish. One could say, I suppose, that I know the mind of these fish because it is like my mind. Thus, I could be sure that you do not know the mind of these fish because you say, standing on the bridge, that the fish are enjoying themselves. And I, knowing what they are really thinking, also know that today they are no happier than any other day. You could not know my mind because you do not know this. It is not at all clear, then, that you have answered my original question. How do you know the fish are enjoying themselves this morning?"

When they had reached the other end of the bridge, Bin Tu turned to the younger monk and opened his hands as if expecting some invisible truth to be dropped there. "Let us go back to where our conversation has begun this morning."

They lingered at the edge of the far side of the bridge, making sure they had not yet set foot on monastery grounds.

"You asked me how I know what brings pleasure to these fish. But you already knew how I knew it when you asked me. You knew that I knew it by standing here on the bridge at the river Po and simply looking at the fish. Indeed, you knew that I knew before we made this morning's journey that has brought us, as it always has, to the other side of the river. If all minds are the manifestation of a single thinker, and if that single thinker has but one thought, then you know how I knew.

"But let us approach the matter your way, as if the mind had sturdy walls in which it were kept. If it is true that I am not a fish and thus am not privy to the thoughts of fish; and if it is also true that you are not me and thus do not know if I am privy to the thoughts of fish; and it is also true that I am not you, and thus I don't know whether you know whether I am privy to the thoughts of fish, then, it seems to me, we are back at our starting point."

Bin Tu looked down again at the darting minnows. "And so, my friend, look at the minnows," he said, "they are particularly happy this morning, don't you think?"

A moment later, the great wooden monastery door swung open on its creaking hinges, and several men dressed in saffron robes silently bowed bidding the two monks a welcome. For the next several hours they would eat a small breakfast and then work in silent prayer in the fields which lined the road. They would perform back-breaking work while never stopping to eat or drink.

They would pray silently from the moment their hoes struck the soil until the master of the monastery with a mallet wrapped in burlap struck the large bell in the center of the monastery compound signaling the end of the day's labors. Again they would file into a small dining hall and eat in silence another small meal of rice, soy meal, and fish. But on the way home, when they reached the bridge over the river Po, with the sun disappearing from the western sky, they would return to their clandestine conversation.

But for now, there were more important things to do.

*To know how to suggest
is the art of teaching.*
H.F. Amiel
Sermons

Chapter 8

The Art of Teaching

The Secrets of College

The secret to doing well in this class is finding
out what the teacher wants and then giving it to him.
Entry on a recent college course evaluation

The secret to college is for a student to find what
she wants from life, and then to go for it.
From the introduction of a college view book for prospective students

ore than a decade ago, upon the publication of my first book, I
embarked on a bus tour that took me to eighty-three cities and
towns in ninety days. In that time and those places I shamelessly
hawked my book with all the zeal and little of the success of a frenet-
ic Fuller Brush salesman. Along the way, I established two rules: first,
stay at the closest hotel to the bus station; and, second, listen to anyone who was willing to talk.

It was on this literary pilgrimage of mine that I came upon one of
the great secrets of life. It was on a midday bus to Kansas City. In a
small town in Idaho a man boarded the bus. His attire marked him as
a man to be reckoned with. On his left foot, he wore a white sneak-
er; on his right, a desert boot. His white pants were held up by a
much larger man's belt. His Hawaiian shirt was stuffed securely into
his underwear which peaked out from the top of his high-water
trousers. What I took to be all his worldly possessions were tucked
away in a disposable diaper box that was held together by copious
amounts of string.

The man surveyed the available seats, and then promptly made
himself at home in the aisle seat next to mine. A moment later, he
pulled from his pocket an old, Japanese, 1960s transistor radio. He

plastered the radio to his left ear, and for a moment stared ahead, as if receiving an important signal. A moment later, the man turned to me and asked in a soft but steady voice, "Do you want to know a secret?"

"Sure," said I.

"God," he said, pausing dramatically, "speaks to me in this radio."

"What frequency is he on?" I asked.

"Oh no," the man replied. "I asked you if you wanted to know *a* secret, not *two* secrets."

And so, it is clear I come to you today as a man who has had his share of secrets revealed to him. And it is in this spirit that I wish to tell you what I have gathered to be the most important secrets to college. I give these to you free of charge. You may do with them what you wish. There are ten secrets in all. I think of them as biblical.

First, you must regain the "Oohh." To fully grasp what this means, you must remember back to how you acted in the first grade when you knew the answer to a question the teacher asked. If you remember, you made a little oohhing sound. It was connected to your elbow which straightened up allowing your arm to shoot up in the air and your mouth to say, "Oohh...Oohh...Oohh..." Now think of how you act when you know the answer in your high school classes. You look left and right for the possibility that there might be witnesses, then you tentatively raise your hand. Sometimes in mid-raising you change your mind, and pretend you are simply playing with your hair. The first secret should be clear: you must regain the Oohh.

Second, don't stare at the desk if you don't know the answer. There is no strange law of physics that essentially says if I cannot see the teacher, the teacher cannot see me. You are too big to disappear. I know it worked for the bogey man, but believe me, it won't work in college.

Third, show up on time. College teachers dislike many things. One of the things they dislike the most is people who habitually show up late. Don't single yourself out as one who does not care. Fourth, don't end up in the weeds in your first semester. There is an interesting story in Plato's *Phaedrus*. It is in this dialogue that he describes the human soul as a chariot, a charioteer, and two horses. One horse runs chaotically, the other runs straight no matter what. The charioteer must use the energy of the wild horse, and the tamer horse's ability to follow a lead, to keep the chariot on the road.

In this little metaphor, the wild horse stands for one's emotions and passions; the tame horse for one's ability to follow orders, even if they do not make sense. If the charioteer allows the chaotic horse to lead the chariot, the first semester freshman winds up in the weeds. It is much more difficult to keep one's chariot on the road in the first semester of college than at any other time.

Connected to this fourth secret is another. Don't call home every night either. Call once a week. Try to give this living on your own thing a chance. Don't let the horse that always does what it's told to lead your chariot.

Fifth, people who are passive in class tend to be seen as under-achievers. If you don't know the answer to a question, take a stab at it. Volunteer before the professor calls on you. You get a good reputation this way, and you also may avoid preemptive strikes. Sixth, find someone trustworthy to whom you can tell your secrets. Most people make some of their best friends in college, be discriminating about who they are.

Seventh, always read your written work out loud before turning it in. If it sounds good, then it probably is. If it sounds clunky, it will sound worse to the teacher. Fix it. And then read it out loud again. Eighth, major in something you love. If you do not, you soon will get bored. Listen to what your parents and friends say about a major, but make sure you pick something you love. Ninth, if you don't have a nickname, invent one. College may be your last chance.

Tenth, don't forget your family, they are worried about you. When you call once a week, don't just ask for money. And finally, an eleventh secret, absolutely free: remember these words of Lilly Tomlin's, "The only problem with winning the rat race is after you've won, you're still a rat."

THE BATTLE OVER ZORGAN

In matters of communication, just as important as what is being said
is the realization of who is doing the saying. Miscommunication so
often happens when we have made a fatal error about the identity of
the person with whom we are, ostensibly, communicating. This fatal
error happens with some regularity.

Michael Polanyi
Essays

When a man does not understand a thing, he feels discord within
himself: he seeks causes for this dissonance not in himself, as he
should, but outside himself, and the result is war with something
he does not understand.

Anton Chekov
The Selected Letters of Anton Chekov

The instructor had handed out the assignment the previous week. He had organized the students into reluctant partners, perhaps the educational equivalent of what some of the teacher's older relatives in less politically correct times used to call a shotgun wedding. But this was to be a wedding of minds. Each pair of students would work cooperatively on a short story. The entire assignment was to be completed on e-mail; it would take no longer than an afternoon. The first student of each pair was to write the opening paragraph of the story, and then e-mail it to his/her partner. The second student would, in turn, write the second paragraph and send it back to the first student who would then construct the third paragraph. They would continue this way until the story was completed. The assignment was to be finished by next week's class.

The instructor had said the assignment was an important one. He had said that it might teach the students something about point of view, the development of character, and the importance of a consistent narrative voice. The instructor had said it would teach the student writers something of the difficulty of what he called "breathing from another's lungs." He had said the students should approach the assignment with a sense of openness and adventure, the way one might try a new food or visit an exotic place, where habit and social identity might be abandoned or at least temporarily misplaced.

The most interesting story of the class began this way, with an opening paragraph provided by the young woman of the pair:

> So Eleanor curled her long legs beneath her and as she watched the steam rise from her steeping tea, her mind drifted to thoughts of Peter. Could relationships really be this difficult? Was it in fact as arduous a task to know the soul and heart of another human being as it now seemed? So much had happened between them, and yet so much had remained unspoken, perhaps hidden just beneath the surface chatter or even the deeper passion.

The young woman put her paragraph through spell-check, then she examined it for split-infinitives and misplaced modifiers, and she sent it on to her waiting partner, a man of approximately the same age, who added this second paragraph:

> Meanwhile...out in the cosmos, unknown to Eleanor, on the planet Zorgan, the evil Zorgonians were planning an assault on the earth that would render insignificant Eleanor's interpersonal difficulties. For in a scant few minutes, Eleanor, Peter, and all the other luckless inhabitants of their doomed planet would be vaporized by the Zorgonian Death Ray. It would be a great victory for Zorgino, their king, a man who had suffered much at the hands of the earthlings. A being as brilliant and cunning as he was ruthless.

The young woman quickly read the second paragraph, her brow furrowing as she moved the cursor down the page. Then spent an hour constructing the third:

> Fortunately, in Eleanor's travels as an astronaut she had befriended the Zorgonians, and, using her special satellite hook up—a present from Zorganus IV, their former king—he brokered a peace treaty just moments before the earth was to be obliterated. The sleek, black Zorgonian space craft returned to its planet, the people of Zorgan again happy and content that they could live harmoniously with their sisters and brothers on earth. With war averted, Eleanor could return to matters closer to home, to important matters of the heart.

To this her male partner confidently appended a fourth paragraph:

> Unfortunately, the Zorgonians were not to be trusted. After making a loop around the earth's moon, they hid there on the dark side, planning their merciless attack. It would be swift and sure. It would be all the more satisfying to Zorgino and his faithful lieutenants, his sadistic henchmen, now that it was a surprise. It would be overwhelming and final. It would be one of the greatest conquests in this or any galaxy.

The woman responded:

> I can't continue this. It is a mockery of the assignment and of literature itself...you have made this very difficult for me...I have tried to cooperate with you, but at every turn you have made it impossible to complete this assignment. You are, simply, an insensitive, macho jerk.

The man immediately shot back:

> And you are a neurotic, whining, self-absorbed, narcissistic navel-gazer.

To this, the woman sent the following message:

Bastard.

To which the man responded:

Bitch.

And so it was that by the end of the afternoon, the pair had completed the assignment with perfect character development. They had accomplished it the way we might try a new food or go on to visit an exotic land.

CONSTRUCTING LARGER HOPES

*A hope, if it is big enough, can bring
defeat as quickly and as thoroughly
as the deepest despair.*
William Bolitho
Camera Obscura

*Memory and hope constantly incite us to
the extensions of the self which play so
large a part in our daily life.*
Josiah Royce
The Problem of Christianity

Teaching. In the morning we will begin again. For twenty-three
Septembers I have been trying to get it right. The night before we
begin, I always have had the same fears, recurring apprehensions.
Why have I been entrusted to do such an important job? Who put me
in charge? Why in this country where there are more educational theories than successes does it not seem so important to others that I do
a good job? And why do I always feel the night before that I will not
be up to the task?

Tonight in preparation for tomorrow's class, I am reading fragments
from the pre-Socratic philosophers—men who lived 2600 years ago in
a remote part of the eastern Aegean Sea. This evening, thanks to my
desk lamp, and a few years in classical Greek class, they are alive. They
are closer to me than my next door neighbor who moments ago has
switched off his reading lamp to retire for the evening. I have been left
with Thales, Anaxagoras, Anaximander, Heraclitus, and Parmenides, a

curious fellow who thought that nothing ever changes, yet devoted his lengthy life to the craft of teaching.

What would these men think of me were they to hear what I will say of them in the morning class? Would they recognize the ideas that moved them to write, and to teach? Would they find odd my attempts at describing their passions? Would they find me lacking as one of the keepers of a tradition that stretches back nearly three millennia?

And what of myself? Will I be able and willing to convey to my students the ideas that move me to write and teach? Will I find a way to convey how important it is to possess a life of the mind? Or will they find me oddly out of step with the way things are?

Tomorrow too many of my students will be there to get their tickets punched. They will be polite and careful, the way sheep are careful around a skilled herd dog. Many of these students are not yet inspired by a great hope, and I wonder if I will be able to point them to places where they might be found.

If I have learned anything in teaching, it is that souls must grow into their proper hopes. This surely is the most difficult part of teaching. It is not the preparation, nor the lecturing; it is not the endless grading of papers, nor the constant gentle cajoling that is as much a part of teaching as chalk dust. The most arduous part of teaching is helping a student find the elasticity in her soul, often in students who have never before been stretched.

Emerson said that passion is not a great regulator, but it is a powerful spring. In the morning I will go in search of passion. I will ask them what it is that moves them. I will ask them about what they think in the middle of the night when the rest of the world is no longer keeping watch. Some will find me odd, intrusive for asking "personal questions." But this must be the first step—to find a passion or two lurking just beneath the surface, passions that might be expanded into larger hopes when the weather turns cold.

Later, around the time we turn to Plato's *Republic*, I will begin to speak to them of patience, and how much of it is required to make larger hopes real. But tomorrow we will begin with Thales—a man with a passion to know what the entire universe was made of. He thought it was water.

I think it was hope.

HUCK DOWN THE RIVER

Hain't we got all the fools in town on our side?
And hain't that a big enough majority in any town?
Mark Twain
The Adventures of Huckleberry Finn

L ast January's issue of *Harpers* brought an article by novelist Jane Smiley in which she expresses a good bit of amazement that Mark Twain's *The Adventures of Huckleberry Finn* is considered by critics to be a great American novel. She goes on at some length to argue that the book should not even be considered a "serious novel," and further that the book achieved its supposed lofty status because of a literary old boys club (white, middle-class male authors). Smiley argues that these critics have exaggerated the book's few virtues, while minimizing or ignoring its many faults, including what she calls a "deeper racism" that permeates the novel.

When I read the *Harpers* piece I was reminded of a lecture and discussion I conducted for second year students at the Johns Hopkins Medical School a few months before Smiley's article appeared. Sitting before me were 125 of the brightest students in America, the distillation of an admissions process that began with over 4,000 applicants, more than half of whom met the necessary entrance requirements. Among those admitted were a dozen African-American students. During the lecture, the black students were seated together in a few front rows. They clearly were agitated by something: by me, by the subject at hand, or perhaps both.

The subject at hand was a small piece of Twain's *Huck Finn*. I had given the students the excerpt as homework. In this part of the book, "You Can't Plan a Lie," Huck and the escaped slave Jim float along on the Mississippi. In a short time, if they make it to Cairo, Illinois, Jim will become a free man.

As their raft moves toward freedom, Huck begins to experience pangs of conscience about helping Jim. Doesn't Miss Watson own the escaped slave? Isn't this like stealing from Miss Watson? Huck, after a tortuous but silent self-examination, decides it would be best to turn in Jim. So the boy leaves the raft, telling Jim he is going to reconnoiter. Moments later, Huck is found by bounty hunters who ask if the raft shrouded in the mist contains a white man or a black man. The young boy swallows hard and says, "White man."

During the class, I attempted to get the students to decide if Huck had done a morally permissible thing in telling the lie. My larger purpose was to help these students eventually to connect the moral ambiguity of Huck's situation with the ethical conundrums and paradoxes that have become a regular part of the practice of American medicine.

The African-American students resisted, not just making a decision about Huck, but in any discussion of the novel at all. After a bit of reluctant probing on my part, they told me it was because this section of the novel contained the N-word. One student went so far as to say that if a text contained the word, then it was, by definition, a racist text.

The Smiley article reminded me of this student's comment, but the *Harpers* piece went on to make a second claim, one that I found odd and interesting—that this country would have been better off if rather than "[A]ll of modern American literature com[ing] from *Huck Finn*, as Ernest Hemmingway once remarked, it had come instead from H.B. Stowe's *Uncle Tom's Cabin*."

Unlike *Huck Finn*, Ms. Smiley writes, Stowe's novel portrays "thoughtful, autonomous, and passionate black characters." Huck's Jim plays the role of a slow-witted straight man. This depiction of Jim, Smiley argues, promotes a "simplistic and evasive theory" of racism that ultimately is to be conquered by just getting along better together.

I found Smiley's view odd because *Huck Finn* is a so much more optimistic book about human nature and the slavery problem than the Stowe novel is. This may well be because *Uncle Tom's Cabin* was completed more than a decade before the Civil War, while *Huck Finn* was finished a generation after the war between the states.

Stowe's book could easily have the reader believe that the only real solution to the plight of mid-nineteenth century American blacks is repatriation to Africa. Indeed, most of the central black characters in the book either return to Africa (George and Eliza), are beaten to death (Tom), or commit suicide (Lucy). In Twain's *Huckleberry Finn*, Jim makes it to freedom, while the two white con-men, the King and the Duke, are caught and run out of town. What appears to be power early on turns out to be mean-spirited nonsense exposed in the nick of time.

I suspect that the real problem my medical school students and Ms. Smiley have with the book comes from not understanding *Huck Finn's* deepest messages. They read the book the way we sometimes criticize conservative Christians of reading the bible. They read and comprehend the book at only the most literal and superficial level. *Huck Finn* is about the adventures of boys on the Mississippi river in the same way that *Moby Dick* is about whaling, or the *Brothers Karamazov* is a detective story.

Many Americans have read Huck Finn in this superficial way for a long time. It was removed from the shelves of public libraries in Boston just days after its publication in 1885. A short time later, various reform schools for boys from Colorado to Flatbush followed suit, calling the book "full of outrageous ideas," and "unfit for young and impressionable minds." These days *Huck Finn* is apt to disappear from public libraries because the book contains words that many people find offensive. Ultimately, removal of *Huck Finn* for this purpose is a gross failure to understand that words, and their capacity to wound or to heal, only make sense in the context in which they are uttered. More importantly, it is a failure to comprehend that *Huck Finn* at its deepest level is a sustained argument against racism. It is a compendium of essential moral values: kindness, loyalty, courage, integrity, and, above all, an unflagging optimism about one's ability to survive in an often hostile and unfeeling world.

The day before my lecture at the Hopkins Medical School, I gave another talk at a middle school in one of the poorest neighborhoods of Washington, D.C. In a class full of African-American twelve year olds, I used the same excerpt from *Huck Finn*. After twenty minutes of talking about Huck's moral dilemma, a small boy with flashing eyes

raised his hand. He went on to inform me, and the rest of the children, that Huck's story was "about my life."

When I ask the boy to continue, the room got unusually quiet.
The boy went on to tell a story about how a few weeks before he had
witnessed a man shot to death on 14th Street.

"When the police come...I tell them I ain't seen nothing...I was
tying my shoes. The way I figure it, Huck had to tell a lie to save a
black man's life. All I was doing was the same thing—telling a lie to
save a black man's life, my own."

DRAGGING A BARN UPHILL

*Clear memory, like nothing else, announces
what is important to us.*
Bertrand Russell
Letters

*Real study, real learning must, for the individual,
be quite valueless or it loses its value.*
Stephen Leacock
Model Memoirs

Memory is a curious and neglected junkyard. Things get dragged
there. They rust or gather dust, or slowly the paint peels in the
hot sun. But sometimes an object is retrieved, brought out of the
jumbled mass of experience, to serve as a metaphor—something from
the past that might help to make sense of a jumbled present.

This morning I stopped my car on a country road. Classes had
ended, a green field was coming to life, and I was in no hurry. There
was an old barn, gray and dry, a hundred yards from the road. In an
instant, I remembered another barn at the foot of the Scottish high-
lands. Years ago while hiking I had stopped to watch a frugal Scot
go about demolishing the ancient wooden structure. Common
practice among farmers in this part of the world was to hitch one's
tractor to the uphill corner post and pull it out until the barn came
tumbling down.

I had arrived in time to watch the reed-thin farmer secure a large
chain to the post. He mounted his tractor and began tugging away,
but the red machine—clouds of gray smoke puffing from its stove
pipe exhaust—did not move. The farmer gritted his yellow teeth and

opened the throttle, until finally, with an awful wrenching sound the tractor began slowly to move. But the farmer did not realize what those of us watching did. Behind him the barn had broken loose from its moorings and was now following him, intact, up the hill.

The work of a teacher is, of course, much like the tale of this Scottish farmer. We spend ten months pulling our students along without much knowledge of our real success. The most stubborn students, when they move at all, make no real internal changes, but they follow you along anyway. Often the trip is uphill.

It did not occur to me until this morning how much of teaching these days requires careful and gentle demolition. In good teaching, one must first pull down structures that will not last, before they can be replaced with something more permanent. It has become increasingly difficult in the last few years to get students to see that not every idea is a good one. We live now in a world of electronic solipsism. Students are often insulated from real experience by the virtual kind. Tabloid television shows now follow the network news, and Jerry Springer is invited to sit at the anchor's desk. Students hand in papers where they footnote conspiracy theories they have gleaned from a chat room on the Internet. When asked the question what is the last book that changed their lives, they usually sit in stunned or dumbfounded silence.

One of the most disheartening effects for those of us who teach is that we now spend much of our time pulling and tugging on children and young adults whose minds have principally been shaped by ideas that last about as long as a tank of gas. There is no longer, for any practical purposes, a lasting notion of a liberal democracy, nor the importance of a rational exchange of ideas in that democracy. We don't argue in polite ways about things that matter.

What I find missing in many of my students these days is the notion of an American polity, an identity that goes beyond the self or one's small ethnic or religious affiliation. We have become in this country a series of smaller and smaller special interests groups, and we have taught our children to think in like ways.

Good societies make demands on their young, while allowing them freedom for frivolity. But frivolity comes these days in pierced body parts and tattoos that, by anyone's standard, will look rather silly when their owners are in their 60s. Short of the Bantu tribes, there is something odd about a society that expresses its individuality by allowing its members to put metal studs through their tongues. It is, perhaps, more disturbing to ponder the degree to which this self-mutilation is a conscious activity.

More than anything, what I find missing in many of my students these days is any reverence for the past. The past for some of them is entirely disposable. It is something we have consumed, so it makes sense to throw it away. These students are pleasant, but they are stubborn. They can't imagine that their minds could be richer or deeper than they already are.

They are like dragging a barn uphill.

Ten Rules of Teaching

*It is nothing short of a miracle
that the modern methods of teaching have
not entirely strangled the holy curiosity of inquiry.*
Albert Einstein
quoted in George Leonard's *Education and Ecstasy*

*I am indebted to my father for living,
but to my teacher for living well.*
Alexander the Great
quoted by Diogenes Laertius in his *Lives*

It is an indisputable fact that Summer ends on Labor Day. We may make lots of noise and throw confetti on the evening of December 31, but anyone who has ever gone to school knows better. The new year begins the day after Labor Day. For the next few days those of us who teach—mostly out of the corners of our eyes—will watch Summer's passing, gone without much fanfare, like innocence or solvency.

None of this Indian Summer stuff for the teacher. Indian Summer: a double misnomer, if ever there were one. There is nothing Indian about it, not North American, nor farther East. It remains Summer only for short order cooks on holiday and stock brokers bereft of children, people who take their vacations when and where they please. These are folks who do not think about September as the beginning of anything, let alone something as momentous like the serious business of teaching and learning.

For as many summers as I can remember (by my count that's nearly forty-nine of them now), I have spent the final weeks of

August usually at the beach, usually brooding about the approaching school year. When I was a child, in August I worried about whether my teacher would like me and whether I would fit in with the kids who seem to matter. For the past twenty-five years—the length of my fledgling teaching career—I have spent the remainders of August wondering about whether my students would like me, and trying, as best I can, to get a handle on what it means to be a person who matters.

This annual trek to the beach is the only time of the year when I do not wear a watch. The daily movement of the sun is the only timepiece one needs. Most of my preparatory thinking about school is done at the water's edge, or, still better, in the Great Sea itself. Against a backdrop of aquamarine timelessness a watch seems superfluous and comical, an odd attempt to exert a kind of control that the sea seems forcefully to argue against.

For the past ten years or so, my musings at the beach have come early in the morning, or on lamp-lit evenings when my small son finally has collapsed. But this year I have spent only two days at the beach. In that time, I spent several hours in the ocean with my young son. Children have always been an extraordinary source of insight. They are often capable of flashes of insight, brilliance unfettered by adult routine.

One Sunday afternoon, while jumping waves with my son, I had another revelatory experience brought to me by this three-foot-ten-inch philosopher with hair the color of straw and eyes that look like tiny green reflecting pools left behind by the sea.

We were holding hands while jumping two to three foot waves. Each wave rolled to a peak, and I would pull the boy's hand, and up we would go. In the best of it, we came to the height of our jump at precisely the crest of the wave. For over half an hour we used this technique, salt spray striking our faces, as I bellowed approval at our considerable skill.

But after a while, it was clear there was something bothering the boy. His arm had lost its muscle. There was no longer enthusiasm in his grasp. A moment later, standing in the water up to his skinny chest, he said this: "Daddy, I am not jumping these waves. You are pulling me over them. When are you going to let me do my own jumping?"

For the remainder of the afternoon, and all the following day, the boy did his own jumping. But this left me with a new set of dilemmas. Do I enjoy my own jumping, or do I cancel my fun to make sure the boy is safe? Just how close do I stay to the boy so that he thinks of it as his jumping, while being close enough to rescue him if he should fail in his judgment of a wave?

These also are the conundrums of a good teacher. How do we lead students by getting them to believe we are simply following? How do we help students who are entrusted to us to act responsibly, while providing a safety net when they do not? How many times should we watch a child fail on her own before we step in? How do we make sure it is their jumping, while taking care that they do not drown?

I do not know the answers to these questions. What I do know is that in my teaching I continually return to a small number of truths about teaching. I offer them here as a kind of ten commandments, knowing full well that I often break them.

First, remember that teaching is too silent a profession. We rarely talk to other teachers about teaching. Most conversations between perfectly good teachers, at all levels, is about gossip. It is permissible and advisable to shame them into talking about teaching.

Second, the surest way to fail a child is to talk disparagingly about her to other teachers. If you find that you spend more than a handful of minutes in a typical week talking about how good your students used to be, and how poor they are now, then you may well be in the wrong line of work.

There is a corollary to this second commandment. No other profession is as proud as we are at a low success rate. "I fail a good 25% of my students," a colleague once proudly proclaimed. Imagine brain surgeons or mail carriers boasting like this, "I kill a good quarter of my patients, they never awaken from the surgery," or "I routinely throw away 25% of the mail I am suppose to deliver." We would find this odd indeed.

Third, we don't ask our students enough about their dreams. We ought to know more about who they are preparing to be. Note I said *who*, not *what*. There is entirely too much emphasis in this country on preparing people for the workplace.

Fourth, we rarely ask our students to verbalize what they think their obligations are to those without the same advantages as they. We don't tell them enough about these obligations when they don't seem to know.

Fifth, much of teaching involves stultifying minutiae. The art of good teaching involves knowing what to overlook. In this regard, the teacher's skills are often closest to those of a good triage nurse in the emergency room. Figure out what needs to be done well, and do it first.

Sixth, self-appropriated learning, self-discovered learning lasts the longest. At least a quarter of all learning must be of this kind, self-initiated. Seventh, never give the same lecture twice. Students know when the lecture notes you are teaching from are looking a little tired and threadbare. This gives students the impression that the stuff they are learning was embalmed many years ago, and is simply dragged out this time every year.

Eighth, there is always at least one kid in the room whom you have misjudged. By the end of the year, you should find her and tell her. It will do her a world of good, and it does little harm to show your students that you can be wrong every now and then.

Ninth, we rarely expect enough of our students. They almost always can do more than they think they can, and usually more than we think they can. You should explain this to them. And finally, tenth, the two most important things about teaching involve passion—a love for one's students and a genuine passion for the subject to be taught. If either of these passions is missing, students know. Pretending to have passion where there is none is always a big mistake.

In a few days we will once again try to do one of the most difficult things on earth, to teach well, and thus to learn well. One of my intellectual heroes, a woman who has taught with imagination and grace for over sixty years, last semester, right before she was to enter her first class of the term, winked at me and said, "Well, let's try to get this right this time." Another of my mentors, a retired professor at the Yale Divinity School, told me in a telephone conversation about ten years ago that the real aim of teaching is "to fail a little more nobly the next time."

Together these scholars have taught for more than a century. They both have a reverence for, and an understanding of, the difficulty of the task. It may well be that our teaching says more about who we are than any other single human activity we might perform. Start fresh, work hard, remember to laugh every now and again, and remember, the rest of us know how difficult it is to do well. Just try to get it right this time. Try to fail a little more nobly the next time.

And good luck.